More Praise for
Choking on the Silver Spoon

Choking on the Silver Spoon offers tim *dling the problems and concerns of today's* *Jeffrey D. Fox, Director of Educational* *Magazine*

D0711715

Parental steps can help rich kids live responsiвly.
Kathy Kristof, *Personal finance Columnist, L.A. Times*

This book offers an important roadmap for careful navigation through the question of outlandish materialism in our children's lives.
Nashville Parent

…the information is thorough and the advice sound for parents of all ages.
Metro Augusta Parent

Buffone's book offers practical ways to handle ones' progeny if they start acting like selfish little brats, sulky teams or greedy adults eager for the will to be probated.
South Florida Parent

Gary Buffone deals with ways wealth affects children.
Publishers Weekly

Bronze Medal Winner, 2004 Annual National Mature Media Awards

While you may want to give your child the world on a silver platter, Dr. Buffone's book will teach you how to responsibly dish it out to them.
Brian M. Johnson, *Physicians Money Digest*

Choking on the Silver Spoon deals with the very serious problem of handling children and money matters in a fair and balanced manner that will not "spoil" children, but rather teach them the true value of hard earned wages, give them initiative to achieve, and help them financially when they are on their own.
Midwest Book Review

Choking
on the
Silver Spoon

GARY W. BUFFONE, PH.D

Choking
on the
Silver Spoon

Keeping Your Kids
Healthy, Wealthy and Wise
in a Land of Plenty

GARY W. BUFFONE, PH.D

Simplon Press
2003

This book includes information from many different sources and is published as a general reference and is not intended to be a substitute for professional financial, legal or psychological advice or consultation. The publisher and author disclaim any personal liability, directly or indirectly, for information presented within. Although the author and publisher have prepared this manuscript with utmost diligence and care and have made every effort to ensure the accuracy of the information contained within, we assume no responsibility for omissions, inaccuracies or errors.

ISBN: 0-9746535-0-0

FOR QUANTITY DISCOUNTS FOR YOUR COMPANY, FIRM OR INSTITUTION for reselling, gifts, incentive programs, fundraising or educational purposes, contact the publisher at Simplon Press, 14653 Marsh View Drive, Jacksonville, Florida, 32250 or the author at www.successpsych.com.

To my girls, Jennifer and Jill
who have been my greatest teachers

Acknowledgements

I wish to sincerely thank:

My wife Norma for her unwavering love and support all these many years, without which this book would not have been possible.

My friend Richard Stoudemire whose brilliant legal mind freed the words you are about to read.

My agent Ken Atchity, of Atchity Entertainment International, for his guidance in navigating the world of publishing.

My publicist Doreen Sabina for her excitement, resourcefulness, and dogged determination in getting the word out on the book.

My assistant Ann Gallaher for her enthusiastic assistance in the final preparation of this manuscript and for all her unwavering efforts in its promotion.

My clients and friends who have provided me with the golden opportunity to share in and learn from their experiences.

My professional colleagues who have so generously discussed their own unique challenges while also providing valuable feedback on this project.

All those parents who have dedicated themselves to raising kids who are emotionally healthy, responsible, and wise.

—Gary W. Buffone
October, 2003

Table of Contents

Part Two:
The Five Immutable Laws of Financial Parenting

Self-Test: Do You Practice What You Preach?
I Can't Hear You: Actions Speak Louder Than Words
Rx #5: Modeling a Healthy Relationship to Money

Part Three:
Living the Laws from Cradle to Grave

When Blood and Business Mix: Passing On the Dream
Making It Work: A Few Family Business Guidelines
Dollar Distributions: How Much Is Too Much?

Questions of the Heart: Talking With Your Financial Advisors
Golden Giving: Smart Moves in the Transfer of Wealth
Getting the Estate Planning Ball Rolling
Protecting Your Money and Your Kids
Trust Funds for the Good, the Bad and the Ugly
Avoiding Inheritance Battles: Communicating What's What
Tips on Holding the Family Money Meeting
Spending Down: The Advantages of Dying Broke
Positive Philanthropy: Giving It All Away
Loving Legacies: The True Measure of Success

Introduction

Whether you chose to accept it or not, you're rich, or at least well off. I know this because the average reader of this book has a household income of around $100,000 or more, putting you in the upper segment of the wealthiest country in the history of the world. It's so easy to lose sight of this fact as we often take our good fortune for granted. So whether your income happens to be a bit less, or much more, you're rich, and a great deal better off than most people on the planet.

Over my many years practicing as a psychologist, I've been fortunate to have met many people like you whose lives have been blessed by economic success, or as historian David Potter has called, "people of plenty." We live in a land of economic and material abundance that has permanently, and often unconsciously, shaped our lives and the lives of our children.

But that doesn't mean that we're all Rockefellers, for the prosperous families I've worked with have come in all shapes and sizes. I refer to these different groups as the future rich, the simply wealthy, and the super-rich. Allow me to introduce you.

The first group, that I refer to as the future rich, are not currently millionaires but will likely become one in the not too distant future. These middle class individuals work and save hard with the ultimate goal to be able to retire some day and live the life they've planned for years. Though not rich in a glamorous sense, they are comfortable and enjoy a reasonable standard of living. Over twenty five million of these traditionally middle class families will inherit small fortunes from their parents and ultimately achieve assets in the range of a few million dollars, accumulating a small, yet considerable estate.

We stand on the brink of a huge intergenerational transfer of wealth that will thrust numbers of such families into the midst of millions. John Havens and Paul Schervish of the Social Welfare Research Institute at Boston College estimate that baby boomers will inherit $41 trillion dollars over the next fifty years, which spread between 76 million boomers, averages out to around $1 million each. Given that most boomers won't be around by mid-century, the next generation stands to fare even better. Think of it as this country's next big gold rush, a new greening of America.

These huge transfers of wealth will propel more and more Americans into the sobering and often contentious business of trying to manage their newfound wealth without ruining themselves or their children in the process. For as the existing affluent have already discovered, more is not necessarily better. More means having more investments, more possessions, more responsibilities, more taxes, more advisors, more dependents, and more to lose. With wealth come new worries and responsibilities.

For many prosperous parents, distributing what they've accumulated ends up being harder than earning it. Responsible parents rightfully worry about how these huge inheritances will affect their children and families. We all know children that become resentful if strings are attached, inheritors that have no idea how to manage money, siblings who feud over who gets what, and "do nothing" adult kids who just hang around waiting for the big "payday." All of this money creates fertile ground for conflict, even in the closest of families.

As a result, it's not just today's wealthy that stand to leave sizable inheritances or face problems in how this will affect their children, it's also those who will assume wealth in the next generations. For the future rich, this money and the associated problems loom just over the horizon. But for the next group, the currently wealthy, many of these issues are today.

So what of the second group, the already rich? The term "rich" has been traditionally reserved for those who are already millionaires, although with inflation and the inevitable fluctuations of the market, this terms means less than it did a few decades ago. Yet, many reading this book either are already millionaires, or like the people just described, have the real potential to have millions in their lifetime.

The amount of wealth in this country may surprise you. In 1988, Kevin Phillips, in his book *The Politics of Rich and Poor*, estimated there to be over 1.5 million millionaires in the country at that time. More current estimates indicate there are over 4.9 million millionaire households among us, although some projections are much higher.

The currently affluent or working wealthy, as artfully described by Drs. Stanley and Danko in *The Millionaire Next Door*, have most often come by their fortunes by owning their own business, working as professionals, conscientiously saving, and most importantly, living below their means.

Although others I have known have become instantly wealthy. These people have come into large sums of money through the sale of a business, inheritance, a big divorce settlement, or in some rare cases, a lucky lottery ticket. In the past decade a number of others have struck it rich in the swirl of corporate mergers, acquisitions, leveraged buyouts and in the old days, dot.com miracles.

These simply rich individuals, whether the working or instantly wealthy, usually have assets in the one to several millions of dollars. Though certainly well off by most standards, their wealth palls in comparison to their more prosperous cousins, the relatively tiny collections of the super-rich.

We are all familiar with the names of the extremely wealthy, although I have only known a few. These more well-known individuals have net worths in the tens to hundreds of millions, to the billions of dollars. You may be surprised to hear that at least several hundred American families fall into this category. Michael Allen offers a fascinating portrait of this country's most affluent in his book, *The Founding Fortunes: A New Anatomy of the Super-Rich Families in America.*

At last count *Forbes* listed over 274 billionaires in the world, more than 100 of whom reside in the United States. We immediately recognize the names of America's brand-name billionaires: Ford, Pillsbury, Rockefeller, DuPont, Pulitzer, Vanderbilt, Hunt, Gates, and the

Mellons. These figures and names immediately instill images of Lifestyles of the Rich and Famous, yet interestingly, some of the super-rich live their lives no more lavishly than their less wealthy counterparts.

All of these individuals, the expectant millionaire, the working or instantly wealthy, the rich and super-rich, appear to have it all. They've all achieved some form of the American Dream.

Yet with all our wealth and privilege, are we really happier, and more importantly, are we comfortable with the effects of our financial success on our kids? Are our children, who seem to have everything, happy and building positive values and self-esteem? Do they have a healthy appreciation for money and "things" and are they willing to work hard to earn them? Have they developed a strong work ethic and sense of personal integrity? Do they handle money responsibly and can they stand on their own two feet economically?

These are the very questions and concerns that plague prosperous parents who often feel sideswiped by the unanticipated effects of their wealth on their children, consequences even the most loving parents are often unprepared to deal with. And for good reason.

The answers to these questions aren't taught in school or offered in even the best business courses. And although there are plenty of books out there on parenting kids and managing money, very few address parents concerns about how wealth negatively impacts their children, particularly adult children, and what parents can do to help them. This book was written just for that purpose, to offer some concrete advice to those parents and families struggling with these complex, and often gut-wrenching issues.

In the first section I discuss the phenomenon of American abundance and outline the inherent dangers families face amidst such good fortune. I provide a specific definition and characteristics of the Silver Spoon Syndrome that clearly illustrates prosperous parents' worst nightmare, that their children will grow up and become spoiled, miserable brats. The section lastly describes what parents truly want for their kids, that they develop a solid sense of self-worth, are financially astute and responsible, and are wise in the ways of the world.

The second section presents the Five Immutable Laws of Financial Parenting, laws that guide parents in making the delicate decisions about their kids and money, regardless of the child's age or stage in life. Throughout this section I provide self-assessment tools to help gauge where parents and children rate on such critical areas as proper discipline, positive motivation, fiscal savvy, and teaching through example.

Lastly, I help parents apply these guiding principles and practices throughout the family life cycle, from teaching youngsters about money with allowances, to launching the reluctant young adult, to fostering a strong work ethic, to tips on the best ways to transfer wealth to the adult child.

So keep reading and you're on your way to protecting your most valuable asset, your children.

PART ONE:

POSITIVE PARENTING
IN THE AGE OF ABUNDANCE

Chapter One

When Wealth Cripples:
The Monetarily Mangled

*Money brings some happiness. But after a certain point,
it just brings more money.*

—Neil Simon

It was the happiest day of his life, or so he thought. When he reached the tender age of eighteen, Jim Martin and his two siblings each inherited ten million dollars from their grandmother's estate. A few short years later, Jim was beginning to understand how sudden affluence can quickly become more cloud than silver lining.

"I've seen money do some ugly things in my family," Jim lamented, "My brother's never worked a day in his life. The money he inherited runs through his fingers like water. He just hangs out and gets high. My sister stays to herself because she doesn't trust anybody. She thinks everybody wants to be with her because of what she has. I've had a hard time staying in school because it's so easy to quit. I don't really have to get up in the morning. I don't have to study hard for tests because I don't have to work, so what's the point?

"My dad fought with my grandmother over her giving us kids all this money. At the time I really didn't see what the big deal was. Who doesn't fantasize about striking it rich? It took me these last few years to understand what my father was so worried about. It's changed our lives forever in ways I never could have imagined. Everybody thinks I've got it made. But sometimes I wish I just had my old life back."

We want to believe in the American Dream. We labor under the cultural delusion that greater wealth equals greater happiness. Buried in this promise of prosperity is the old truth that money may pay the bills, but it confers neither meaning, nor satisfaction, nor love to our lives. Rich and poor alike, we find ourselves trapped in the assumption that more is always better, yet true contentment remains perpetually out of our reach.

People like Jim tell us that money is not an instant recipe for happiness—in fact, it generates special challenges all its own. As another of my clients put it, "Everybody thinks we live this fantasy life: great homes, expensive cars, private schools, extravagant vacations. They don't see the flip side: the long conversations into the night about how money will impact our lives, our kids' lives, our grandkids' lives…people who have never faced these things can't understand how money could ever feel like a curse instead of a blessing."

Jim represents just one example of a group of seemingly advantaged kids cut-off from life's traditional responsibilities and rewards. Lacking conventional ambition and having not yet developed a core identity or purpose, they find themselves lost and disoriented. Without normal goals and solid peer and family relationships as anchors, they are driven to a "special", yet twisted view of reality, and finally to despair.

That's usually where I come in. For over two decades I've been successfully helping people solve their personal and family problems. As a clinical psychologist, I've developed a specialty of solving problems relating to family businesses and fortunes. I've guided the entitled adolescent and the underachieving young adult, I've counseled the stalled careerist, helped select the successor to the family business, and aided parents facing decisions about their ne'er-do-well heirs.

In researching this book, I've also interviewed over fifty financial and mental health professionals to learn of their experiences with wealthy families. I've spoken with brokers, tax and probate attorneys, psychiatrists, accountants, insurance advisors, financial planners, psychologists, church counselors, clergy and family therapists.

I've added to the things they've told me by studying the ways many of our country's wealthiest families have handled difficult financial issues—where they've succeeded and where they've failed.

They all paint a dangerous picture.

Wealth is a double-edged sword. Its unique challenges *can* be mastered, but where they are not handled adeptly, the damage is devastating. And no one pays a greater price than our children.

I've written this book for the parents of these at-risk or troubled children. They have watched helplessly as their beloved offspring develop disturbing attitudes and frightening patterns of behavior. They may or may not connect their financial success to their children's difficulties, but they know that something is going terribly wrong with their youngsters' development. Or, they may have observed other people's children in the throes of the "Silver Spoon Syndrome" and vowed grimly that their progeny will not suffer the same fate. Whatever the case, this book can help.

Within the following chapters, I'll detail the symptoms and causes of the so-called "Silver Spoon Syndrome," or "affluenza," as it's sometimes known. I'll also introduce you to a five-step rescue plan that appears here for the very first time in print. I developed this regimen from two decades' worth of successful outcomes in my clinical practice. Once you've understood and applied these Five Laws of Financial Parenting, you'll be armed with specific actions you can take to minister to your children's particular symptoms. You'll learn how to disrupt their dysfunctional patterns of behavior and guide them toward a healthier relationship with money—-and with the world at large.

But before we can collect our weapons to go into battle, we must be very clear about the nature of the beast. We must take a hard look at material wealth, and understand the crippling effect it can have on our kids.

Why Parents Worry: The Ravages of Riches

Let me be clear. Money, even money newly acquired, doesn't always mess up families. I'm pleased to report that, at least in my experience, it adds to the happiness of most. Money itself is never the problem. It's what we do with money that can wreak havoc in our lives.

Money only creates misery when it falls into the hands of those ill prepared to handle it.

The issues we'll talk about aren't solely problems of the rich. Any of us can get into trouble with money based purely on what we believe. It's as much about the mailman who fritters away his opportunities for contentment fantasizing about "striking it rich" as it is about the prosperous physician whose life is void of meaningful relationships and filled with nothing but work and the accumulation of material goods. It includes the dual-career, middle-class couple whose children spend most of their time in the company of strangers—not because the parents need the money, but because they believe more of it is always better.

All of these dysfunctional beliefs about money are learned. Many are passed down from generation to generation. To compound the problem, commercial messages bombard us daily, reinforcing the false notion that material goods are the solution to all our woes. In a society as affluent as ours, individuals at any income level can fall prey to the siren song of wealth.

None are so gravely affected by money as those who have had it dropped in their laps. Recall Jim Martin and his siblings, whose inheritance changed their lives:

"I wasn't raised like some Little Lord Fauntleroy," he told me, "Even though my dad's parents had a lot of money, my parents did a good job of raising us like everybody else. I raked leaves and shoveled snow for money. I didn't get any extravagant toys or gifts. I lived a pretty normal life until I turned eighteen. After the inheritance, everything changed.

"All of a sudden I didn't need to go to work, go to school, or do anything. I quit my job at the grocery store and flunked out my first year in college. It's been difficult figuring out what to do next. I feel like I'm standing in a huge wide open space and I can walk in any direction," he concluded, "But there's no sign to tell me which way to go."

Jim was experiencing a classic case of rich-kid disease, of being "soft where we are hard," as F. Scott Fitzgerald put it in his story *The Rich Boy*. When so much is free, rich kids don't know what to value, or how to obtain what can't be bought. In Jim's case, he had lost all desire and direction. This is why so many young inheritors express a sense of emptiness, depression, and listlessness. Their lives lack any clear purpose.

Nelson Aldrich, in his book *Old Money*, spoke of this dilemma: "The inheritor is placed in the unique position of being able to choose whether to participate in purposeful activities or do nothing at all. Because they are not forced into participation, they often don't take risks, stretch themselves, or connect in a meaningful and instructive way with others. They end up leading an isolated life, lacking in the richness and complexity of experiences."

Jim and countless other young heirs frequently become resentful of their benefactors: "Even though I should be grateful for what my grandmother gave me, I sometimes regret that she didn't use better judgment. I've thought about giving it all away just to get my old life back."

Peter Collier and David Horowitz, in their book *The Rockefellers*, found that many of the famous family's descendants were miserable because of their money. "Most of the fourth Rockefeller generation have spent long years with psychiatrists in their efforts to grapple with the money and the family," say the authors, "To some degree, they are all princes and princesses yearning to be paupers."

John Sedgewick, in his book *Rich Kids*, warns of the hazards of money: "It is like some magic sword: it gives the holder rare powers, but only the mightiest warriors can keep from being nicked themselves by the blade." Jessie O'Neill of *The Golden Ghetto*, and Burton Wixen of *Children of the Rich*, both describe the potential devastation caused by wealth and privilege.

I've worked with both children and adults who have been slashed by the sword of affluence. Some had gaping wounds. Some were literally near death.

Then there are the more dramatic, well-known casualties of affluenza. We all recall the Menendez brothers who murdered their parents to gain access to their estate, McCauley Culkin's family destroyed by his sudden wealth and fame, and the murder and fraud case of the Billionaire Boys Club, to name a few.

Now stop and reflect on your own situation. What delicate issues have you faced in your own life involving money and love? Have you felt guilty for trading more income for time with your family? Maybe you're worried about the effects of buying toys for your kids every time you go to the store.

If you're reading this book, the odds are that you've recognized the warning signs in your own kids. Is your brilliant young son inexplicably flunking out of school? Does your teenage daughter refuse to work then demand her allowance early so that she can go to a rock concert? Or maybe your youngest won't talk to you because you won't buy him the red BMW he wants. Perhaps your grown child doesn't call anymore because she's angry that she's not receiving what she feels she "deserves" from your estate. Does your heart break, hearing your adult kids fighting over what they will get after you die? Or were your hopes dashed when your grown daughter spent your last cash gift on drugs and clothes?

If you've encountered situations like these, you know the guilt, anguish, disappointment and anxiety of watching a child slip into the throes of affluenza. These experiences represent the dark side of wealth, the pitfalls of prosperity, the ravages of riches. Let's take a closer look at the way this vicious cycle of destructive behavior, the Silver Spoon Syndrome, manifests in our children.

In the Shadow: Recognizing the Silver Spoon Syndrome

What is this pernicious Silver Spoon Syndrome that robs our children of their potential for success and happiness? How can we identify it?

I define the Silver Spoon Syndrome as a specific set of attitudinal and behavioral symptoms, resulting from an inappropriate relationship with money and material wealth, that significantly interferes with an individual's ability to function socially, occupationally, and in several other important areas of their lives.

An individual suffering from Silver Spoon Syndrome displays *at least three* of these core traits:

Core Traits of Silver Spoon Syndrome

- **Persistent Underachievement:** lacking motivation, ambition, and drive.

- **Low Frustration Tolerance:** acting out behaviorally or emotionally when told no, unable to delay gratification.
- **Narcissistic Entitlement:** expecting rewards without effort.
- **Fiscal Illiteracy:** failing to handle money responsibly.
- **Distorted Values:** overvaluing or undervaluing material wealth.

These five symptoms form the heart of the syndrome. They usually develop in early childhood and become increasingly acute throughout adolescence and young adulthood. Few individuals will show *all* the symptoms, but the more signs you recognize, the more likely it is that your child is a bona-fide Silver Spooner.

Let's keep in mind that a certain degree of these traits are *normal* in adolescent children. But they are usually shed with further age and maturity. Unfortunately, some people get stuck in this developmental phase, and never grow further unless prodded by external forces. Even then, they go kicking and screaming.

Joyce LeBeau first labeled this syndrome, noting that it is characterized by "chronic mild depression, emptiness, boredom, lack of empathy, high pursuit of pleasure, disinterest in work of any kind, and an overriding belief that money will solve any problem." These children experience a "low sense of nurturance;" in other words, they do not feel loved.

LeBeau states that syndrome sufferers possess an inflated regard for "public self" and a low regard for "private self," resulting from wealthy parents who "consistently choose outward form over the child's legitimate emotional and developmental needs."

Although we're using an "illness" analogy to describe the Silver Spoon Syndrome, we must always keep in mind that the syndrome is not a disease but *a learned pattern of behavior.* The syndrome is *not* caused by wealth—as evidenced by the fact that it can occur in children of any income level—but *by the substitution of material indulgence for critical nurturing.* In other words, children develop the syndrome when they are given things instead of firm, loving parenting.

Now, obviously parents don't do this to their children on purpose. In fact, the Silver Spoon Syndrome is most often a result of good intentions: the parents want a high-quality life for their children, and they mistakenly place too much emphasis on giving them a *materially* good lifestyle while neglecting the nonmaterial parental gifts which no money can buy. Unfortunately, without nurturance and guidance, the glut of material things brings the child not happiness but emptiness, listlessness, and frustration.

It is painfully easy for busy parents in today's world to get caught up in the frenzy of careers and consumerism and to lose sight of the intangible blessings which only they can bestow: love, guidance, discipline, character, values—and the one thing that makes the conferral of these gifts possible, their *time*. Before we even realize it is happening, our children may begin to display the telltale signs of Silver Spoon Syndrome.

Are you concerned that your child may be developing into a Silver Spooner? The following test is a preliminary symptom-check:

Self-Test: How to Spot Them. Is Your Child a Silver Spooner?

Answer Yes or No to the following:

1. Is your child an underachiever, unwilling to work for anything?
   Yes   No
2. Do your children act out emotionally when they don't get their way?
   Yes   No
3. Does your child expect to get things without having to work for them?
   Yes   No
4. Does your child lack the basic knowledge and skills to be fiscally responsible?
   Yes   No
5. Do your kids need to have the latest toys, designer clothes, or status-symbol vehicles in order to feel good about themselves?
   Yes   No

Score two points for each Yes; zero points for each No. Tally your scores, and read on:

Question One: Persistent Underachievement: Affluent parents often worry that their fortunes will destroy their children's ambition. They fear that their kids will lack the motivation, drive, and "stick-with-it-ness" they'll need to accomplish long-term goals. They have reason to be concerned: persistent underachievement is an all too common problem in children who grow up in well-to-do families.

Children afflicted this way complain of feeling bored and listless. They feel lost, without a sense of direction in their lives. These Silver Spooners live from moment to moment, often missing an overarching sense of purpose.

"I just don't understand Mike," shared a frustrated father, "No matter what we do, he won't make any effort at school. I almost killed myself making good grades to get through medical school in order to get where I am today. Mike doesn't seem to care about anything. Even being kicked out of school doesn't phase him."

Mike, like many other affluent children, has motivational problems because he has never learned the relationship between effort and reward. Where Mike's dad had to work for what he wanted, Mike was given everything. Mike had no particular reason to care whether or not he was kicked out of his third private school. It just meant moving back home for a while, where he could hang out with his friends. He had no particular incentive to strike out on his own.

Question Two: Low Frustration Tolerance: If your children are beyond the age of three and still cry, scream, hit, threaten or pout when they don't get their way, you've got a problem. If they're not yet learning to handle their feelings, their low frustration tolerance will set them up for bigger problems down the road.

Children with a low tolerance for frustration have difficulty delaying gratification. Silver Spooners want things when they want them, and become easily agitated when their demands aren't met immediately. At the first sign of obstacles or adversity, they freak.

Billy had been trained to expect things "his way" since he was a young child. Now that he had reached his early teens, Billy's behavior was spiraling out of control. Referred to me by his second school counselor, his parents sat in my office, meekly wondering what went wrong: "The teachers told us we need to discipline Billy, but we're scared to say much because he gets so mad. He's threatened to hit us. We don't know what to do."

Question Three: Narcissistic Entitlement: If your children act as though the world owes them, without any reciprocity on their part, they've developed this classic Silver Spooner trait. Children who exhibit this symptom are commonly called "spoiled."

Psychiatrist Robert Coles, in his book *Children of Crisis: The Privileged Ones*, found that virtually all wealthy families communicate a message of entitlement to their offspring. The message these children receive is, "I have a right to money, power, and status purely by virtue of my birth, rather than by achievement."

"Despite their specialness, their wealth and privilege," Coles writes, "They are unhappy, dissatisfied and empty…The child has much but wants and expects more—only to feel no great gratitude, but a desire for yet more… Underneath there lies apprehension, a gloom and, not least, a knowing sense of worthlessness."

These privileged children become so totally absorbed in fulfilling their own needs that they lack any empathy for the needs and feelings of others, frequently leading to the exploitation of people and relationships. Other people see these narcissistic Spooners as socially noxious. This trait becomes toxic to relationships and prevents the person from developing intimate connections. As their privileged upbringing often shelters these children from real-world consequences, their behaviors are seldom, if ever, challenged.

Question Four: Fiscal Illiteracy: Children who grow up with plenty of spending cash frequently develop an "easy come, easy go" philosophy toward money. As a result, they never learn the basic skills of money management. They develop a taste for some of the "finer things"—designer clothes, high-tech gadgetry, exotic travel, cocaine—and quickly blossom into Big Spenders. They have no concern for the way money works, because there's always plenty. They bounce checks, overextend their credit, and seldom pay their bills. They cannot comprehend the idea of living within their means, because they assume that the means are limitless.

When they do get in trouble, they simply wait for their parents or trust officers to bail them out, then they go happily about the business of spending again. As long as the cash holds out, they never have a motivation to learn better money management habits.

Question Five: Distorted Values: Children who grow up in the midst of ever-plentiful cash may develop an exaggerated relationship to the value of the dollar. They may overvalue it, believing it means everything, or undervalue it, assuming that it means nothing.

Kids whose self-esteem depends on *what they have* rather than *who they are* risk grave problems later in life. They have confused their self-worth with their net worth. These children place an inappropriate value on money, believing that more money makes them a better person. They may also believe that money can buy other intangibles such as friendship, love, meaning, or happiness.

Children who have never seen the connection between work and money may swing toward the opposite extreme. Where money has no value, children spend it recklessly, assuming that there's plenty more where that came from.

Either trait sets the child up for a rude awakening when—and if—they ever venture out into the real world.

Understanding Your Score:

If you scored 0-4: your children are doing pretty well. They don't seem to be showing many of the cardinal signs of the Silver Spoon Syndrome.

A score of 6-8: suggests that your child is developing some problem areas. Look at the questions you answered with a "Yes"— you'll want to pay special attention to the chapters that treat those particular symptoms.

A score of 8 or above: indicates that your kids are spoiled rotten and headed toward developing a full- blown Silver Spoon Syndrome. Don't despair! It's never too late to set a correction course for kids in trouble.

If you're living with a Silver Spooner, you know firsthand that they're unhappy. But as the Spooner's syndrome progresses it brings with it a host of undesirable secondary, or spillover characteristics and effects, including the following:

Shallow, unstable relationships: A true Spooner relates to others primarily from a motive of self-gratification: what can this person do for me? Individuals in relationships with Spooners commonly lament, "It's all about them." The stability of the Spooners' relationships is largely dependent on having others gratify their needs. When they're not getting what they want out of a relationship, the other person becomes quickly disposable, like a used soda bottle.

"At first, Ted seemed so charming and caring," a teenage client lamented of her privileged boyfriend, "I thought he was different from his parents. It took me only a few months to see how pretentious his family was and how they only related to people that could promote their image in the community. They were big into appearances. And as it turned out, Ted was no different. I finally figured out he was only interested in me because I was attractive. As soon as he met a girl he thought was more beautiful, he traded me in like a old car."

Moving from one relationship to another on a whim, Spooners develop little loyalty, commitment, or depth in their connections with others. They monopolize conversations and become quickly bored when the spotlight shifts to someone else. Other people see them as haughty, arrogant, selfish, disdainful and patronizing. Silver Spooners constantly alienate those around them.

Their interactions with others are forever tainted by suspicion: is this person interested in me or in my money? Rich kids are constantly left to size up strangers: how would this person react to me if he knew I was loaded? This self-doubt leaves the affluent child feeling isolated, fearful, lonely, and at times even paranoid. Self-doubt becomes a major obstacle to ever developing true intimacy in relationships.

For this reason, many wealthy children try to quietly blend into the mainstream by concealing their identities. They dress down, drive old cars, hide their past travels and ivy-league educations, and keep quiet about their spending, all to avoid the alienation that wealth sometimes brings.

Ellen Malcolm, the granddaughter of one of the founders of IBM, has experienced the pain money can bring to relationships. She avoided telling her office colleagues about her family: "I thought they would see me as a walking dollar sign instead of the person I am."

Poor self-esteem: Does being well off give children a sense of well-being? In a word, *never.* Silver Spooners often lack a consistent sense of self-worth. They miss out on the meaningful work and deep relationships that help their less affluent peers to feel good about themselves. George Pillsbury, scion of the flour family, once remarked, "It's hard to build self-esteem if you don't deal with the challenge of getting a job."

The Silver Spooners' wealth shelters them from the real-life adversity that puts genuine fiber in young people's backbones. Without it, their emotional growth and development become stunted.

Much of what the Spooners have learned to feel as self-esteem is not the real thing at all, but an external substitute made up of wealth and possessions. Their behavior is often marked with flashy lifestyles and conspicuous consumption designed to impress others.

The phrase "self-esteem" as I've used it here demands further explanation. In recent decades it's been so overused that it's lost much of its meaning. Popular culture has adopted it as a "wastebasket term," to mean every possible permutation of "feeling good about one's self." This is a dangerous misconception. A hearty snort of cocaine will make you feel good about yourself, for a short period of time. But it has nothing to do with self-esteem.

I define self-esteem as the capacity to understand, accept and love ourselves for who we are.

Individuals who possess real self-esteem know it's the genuine article because it's been tested—and has passed with flying colors. It can *only* come from overcoming challenges, from building weaknesses into strengths and holding fast to integrity, discipline and principles in the face of temptations. Only real-world experiences can create true, adult self-esteem: pursuing goals, acquiring job skills, advancing a career, building a business, maintaining a relationship, earning trust.

Less affluent children are forced to face such experiences; their survival demands it. But the child of wealth may never be thrust into the midst of these emotional muscle-builders.

Inflated Sense of Self: Snobbishness is one of the more obvious—and most obnoxious—characteristics of the Silver Spooner. This is not at all contradictory to "low self-esteem," as it may first appear. Often masking deep feelings of insecurity, Spooners are boastful and pretentious. They elevate their own importance while devaluing the contributions of others.

When privileged children are treated as though they are better than others, they grow to expect this deference from the world at large. Like royalty of old, they see themselves as being beyond the ken of ordinary, common folk. They expect to be catered to, and are astonished, even furious, when they don't get the royal treatment.

As a result, Spooners often come to believe that rules were made for other people and don't apply to them. Their disregard for rules can bring them into serious conflicts with authority at school and work—and may even land them in trouble with the law.

Mood Problems and Substance Abuse: Not surprising given the traits we've just mentioned, Spooners are particularly vulnerable to depression and moodiness. They frequently "medicate" their unhappiness with food, alcohol, and drugs—and quickly become dependent on these external substances to avoid the unpleasantness in their lives.

The Spooners' wealth can exacerbate their addictions. My client Jim worried that his brother Greg had thrown himself into a dangerous cycle of sex, alcohol and overspending in order to avoid growing up: "From the outside, it's got to look like the guy has a charmed life. No matter how much trouble he gets into, he's got an army of lawyers and bankers ready to bail him out. But that's just the problem: somebody's always there to rescue him, so he never hits bottom. He never has to face the giant cesspool he's made out of his life, so he never feels like he has to clean it up."

Emotional and Economic Dependency: Like well-dressed beggars, Spooners fall into a pattern of helplessness. They rely on others to provide for their needs. They may resent their dependency on wealthy family members, but they seldom break this destructive cycle.

Psychiatrist Frank Pittman refers to this scenario as the "cozy nest." His research on wealthy families revealed that these dependent Spooners seldom leave home. If they do, they never venture far from the nest. They remain perpetual children, locked in a symbiotic dependency with their controlling parent. Emotionally crippled, they are unwilling to make the necessary sacrifices to separate from the "nest." They never achieve mature independence or adult autonomy.

These, then, are the core and secondary characteristics of the Silver Spooner. Let's see how the syndrome manifests according to such variables as age, socioeconomic level, ethnicity, gender and generation:

Does the Syndrome vary according to age? Its effects grow more pronounced as a child approaches adulthood. As children begin to take on adult tasks, it becomes obvious that they're missing the necessary skills to handle them. It's normal for young children to have a low tolerance for frustration, just as it's normal for adolescents to display a certain amount of narcissism. But the older a child gets, the clearer it becomes that something is amiss. The syndrome often continues into adulthood and, sadly, may persist throughout an individual's life. The more a person is insulated from genuine life experiences, the more likely their Silver Spoon characteristics will become permanently ingrained. Once Spooners reach their forties, the odds of turning their attitudes around diminish rapidly.

Does the Syndrome vary according to social class? Surprisingly, very little. Any or all of the symptoms can be present, to any degree, at any socioeconomic level. I have noticed one exception: the wealthier the family, the more pronounced the Spooner's Narcissistic Entitlement is likely to be. Wealthy families often confer a sense of "specialness" upon their children, whether they do so consciously or not.

Obviously, the more money Spooners have at their disposal, the more excessive their self-indulgence will be. It's easy to see that the greater the wealth, the greater the temptation to err in its use, and the more glaring and public the errors. Too much money, like too much alcohol, simply makes the stupid more stupid.

The most significant difference that I see between an upper-middle-class Spooner and a child of the super-wealthy is in the size of the "cushion" that pads them from real-world experience. The less well-off kid is more likely to get hit with a reality sandwich at some point in his life—and it will most likely come at an earlier age. Wealthier Spooners may spend a lifetime buying their way out of jail, and into a series of private schools. The middle-class Spooner is actually luckier, in the long run, than his better-heeled counterpart: he will probably "bottom out" at some point and be forced to grow from the experience. The richer the kid, the more likely his or his parent's money will insulate him from true growth forever.

So, in short, parents of any socioeconomic level can spoon-feed their children until they "choke"—but the wealthier have a bigger spoon.

Does the Syndrome vary according to gender? If you line up an equal number of well-to-do male children and female children, you'd probably find about the same number of Spooners in each group. But even in this age of increasing gender equality, we still hold very different expectations for each gender. I've had far more parents come to me begging for help with their *sons* than with their daughters.

Particularly in more traditional families—as many of the most affluent are—males are expected to take the reins of the family, to show leadership and ambition. A leavening of propriety still lingers from past generations, when it was considered an upper-class privilege to have one's wife and daughters remain "ladies of leisure."

Male Spooners come in for harsher judgment, particularly because they're more likely to be tapped for succession in the family business. Women, on the other hand, may still get a pass if they decide to raise a family, pursue charitable work, or dabble in the arts. The guilt and shame that a male Spooner generates is still greater than that created by his female counterpart.

Does the Syndrome vary according to generation? You bet it does. The syndrome more commonly develops in the children of "new money," whose parents, understandably, were not prepared to deal with the unique challenges of wealth. It's particularly acute among young heirs, who have vast fortunes dumped in their laps before they've made their own way into the real world. But it can quickly snowball from there: Spooner parents may pass on their mistakes to their children, who compound them with mistakes of their own. In this way, the Syndrome can magnify as it is passed down from generation to generation.

Does the Syndrome vary according to ethnicity? In my experience, only in as much as it's tied to generation. In studying the biographies of America's wealthy families, I came across a common lament: those families who immigrated to this country and built their fortunes struggled to instill their native values in their children, only to despair as their children quickly became Americanized. They saw their cherished cultural values and traditions wash away in the deluge of new cultural influences.

Of course, when we look at any group, we must account for substantial differences in home life, values taught and instilled, beliefs advocated, and so forth. Any generalization may only be taken so far.

These, then, are the Silver Spooners: Narcissistic, emotionally stunted spendthrifts, forever brandishing their credit cards in search of the precious things which money can never buy, often living in a haze of substance abuse from which they may never escape, languishing in a developmental twilight between childhood and adulthood.

They are not happy people.

But there's another factor I have yet to place into this equation. Spooners, as we've discussed, can be born of any income level, but they are particularly prevalent in upper-middle class families and the wealthy. Now, when you realize that affluence is on the rise and good, old-fashioned bootstrapping is on the wane, we'd better brace ourselves for more and more encounters with hard-core Spooners, because within the next few decades, we'll be seeing a lot more of them.

Knee-Deep in Spooners: The Rising Tide of Wealth in America

Despite the cautionary tales of the rich and miserable, America hasn't lost its obsession with wealth. Authors Thomas Stanley and William Danko, in their best-selling book *The Millionaire Next Door*, tell us that during the next ten years the affluent population in America will increase five to seven times faster than the general household population. This wealthy group will produce children and grandchildren, leaving the largest generation of wealthy heirs the world has ever seen. Never before in the history of humankind will so many people face the unique challenges that prosperity brings.

We're not prepared.

For many families, wealth is just a matter of time. We stand on the brink of a huge intergenerational transfer of wealth that will thrust vast numbers of families into the midst of millions. As I mentioned earlier and bears repeating, John Havens and Paul Schervish of the Social Welfare Research Institute at Boston College estimate that "baby boomers" will inherit over $41 trillion dollars by mid-century and then transfer even larger estates to their children. This is a tremendous flood of wealth that could swamp even the healthiest of families. I don't believe we are adequately prepared for this country's next big gold rush, and what it will bring: *A bumper crop of Silver Spooners.*

The Peril of the Spooner Generation: Why We Must Rescue Them

What will happen to our Silver Spooners if we don't intervene?

Joyce LeBeau describes the case of a young adult named Arthur, who graduated high school at age 18 with the highest SAT scores in his class, but who, despite his intellectual talents, failed to gain admission into any college. "Despite a lavish lifestyle of private schools, wonderful vacations, computers, VCRs, a pool, cars, Arthur feels depressed, lonely, and under-nurtured. He entertains grandiose notions of his ability and potential, but falls short in reality because he has no training, structure, or real guidance. Recently he had four car accidents, and after each one his parents immediately bought him a new car, no questions asked. They recognize that he is troubled, but see no causative relationship to them or their lifestyle."

Arthur may never know the unique, magnificent man he could have become. Without our intervention, the Spooners face a stunted, passionless, shadowed half-life. Their lives are likely to be fraught with depression, frustration, desperation and substance abuse. They will probably ache for meaningful, long-term relationships, for a sense of accomplishment, for a reason to get up each day and go on living. Their lives may be but a hollow mockery of what they might have been. They will be miserable, and for as long as they live, they may never figure out how to escape the chasm of emptiness in their souls.

No parents could want this for their children.

This is a tragic scenario, but the picture grows even bleaker when we recognize that these legions of underdeveloped Silver Spooners are the leaders, thinkers, creators and laborers of tomorrow. Some day, the reins of our nation will be in their hands. If they don't receive the necessary tools, they will have nothing with which to build their skills, their talents, their unique contributions to the world. It's a terrible waste of people. Our nation will be the lesser for it.

But how can we stop this Spooner epidemic, when we don't understand how it started in the first place? Were we so wrong to give our kids a more comfortable childhood than we had? If it's not the money itself that saps their ambition and ruins their character, what *is* causing it?

In the next chapter, we'll lay the groundwork for curing our Spooners by examining how they got this way in the first place.

Chapter Two:

Money Can't Buy Them Love: Why We Give Kids Everything Except What They Really Need

A fortune is usually the greatest of misfortunes to children. It takes the muscles out of their limbs, the brain out of their heads, and the virtue out of their hearts.

—Henry Ward Beecher

How the Best Intentions Can Produce the Worst Results

When you ask parents what they want for their children more than anything else, their first response is always, "I want them to be happy."

What exactly is happiness anyway?

To happiness researchers, it is a state of mind: a pervasive feeling that life is good. Social psychologist David Myers reviewed thousands of recent scientific studies conducted worldwide in search of the key to happiness. In his thought-provoking book, *The Pursuit of Happiness,* he explodes many of the myths surrounding the subject of contentment and satisfaction. One such myth has to do with the notion that our sense of well-being comes from being well off. We assume that the more money we acquire, the happier we'll be. But we're setting ourselves up for a grave mistake.

Just How Much Happiness Can You Buy?

When asked in a Roper survey how happy we Americans were with different aspects of our life, we expressed the least satisfaction with the amount of money we have to live on. When a group of University of Michigan researchers asked what hampers our ability to live a good life, the most frequent answer was, "not enough money." Except for those with the highest incomes, most of us thought that a little more money would bring us greater happiness.

But if financial success equals bliss, then we would expect that our satisfaction level would grow with our paychecks: more money, more happiness. Let's look at the numbers.

Since the 1950s the buying power of the average American consumer has more than doubled. In 1957, as John Galbraith was writing his popular book on us, *The Affluent Society,* our per-person income expressed in today's dollars was about $9,000 a year. Today it's $20,000. Compared to 1975, we own twice the number of cars, eat out twice as often, and enjoy a never-ending array of VCRs, home computers, dishwashers, pools, answering machines, juicers, garage door openers, cell phones, and digital personal assistants.

So with this much more income, and all this cool stuff, are we happier?

We are not. In a large survey conducted by the University of Chicago's National Opinion Research Center, the number of people reporting that they were "very happy" declined between 1957 and 1998, from 35% to 33%. In fact, judging from the post-war rise in depression over the same period, we're more likely to be miserable. Psychologist and researcher Martin Seligman reports that depression rates have increased tenfold in the last fifty years.

Over the past four decades, we've become more than twice as rich, yet we are far less happy.

When I think back nearly twenty-five years, when I had just received my doctorate, I was earning about $15,000 a year as a psychologist at a publicly funded mental health clinic. I drove a used VW Scirocco, lived in a hovel near the beach, ran, rode bikes, surfed, played tennis, and hung around with a great set of friends. It was a simple, good life.

Now I earn a strong multiple of my earlier income, have collected considerable assets and "stuff," live in a beautiful home, drive a Lexus, and hold a respectable position in a successful psychological consulting practice. I still run, surf, play tennis and ride bikes, and am also married with two grown daughters starting their own lives. I'm still fortunate to have a great group of friends. Am I happier? Perhaps just a little. But I would say the difference is largely due to my wife and kids and not so much the advances I've achieved financially.

I don't mean any of this to sound anti-materialistic. I enjoy the conveniences and luxuries of our affluent society as much as the next person. Still, for each of us, there's a point of diminishing returns. With our needs comfortably met, more money only buys things we don't need and hardly care about. If we hoard it, it becomes nothing more than a blip on some distant bank computer, a string of digits on a brokerage report. What's the point?

I'm sure we all know, at least on some level, that money can't buy happiness. Yet, with the best of intentions, this is precisely what many parents try to do.

"We Just Wanted Them to Have It Better Than We Did"

In my practice I've counseled hundreds of parents who rose to wealth from modest means. They sweated blood to get where they are today. They lived on Ramen noodles for years. They worked their internships by day, washed dishes in the evenings, and studied half the night away. They struggled, sacrificed, took risks—and prospered. The material comforts they enjoy today are precious to them, because they know, intimately, what it means to do without them, and what it took to earn them.

Can anybody blame them for wanting to spare their children that hardship?

These baffled parents come to me with pain in their eyes. They have proudly given their young sons and daughters the fruit of their labor, only to find that it means nothing to them.

"Jeez, I'd have given my eye teeth for the kind of opportunities my son has," goes the common lament, "I would have raked leaves and mowed grass until my blisters had blisters. But nothing will get this kid off the couch!"

These parents, like all of us, made understandable mistakes. Out of their own desire to give their children something "better" than what they had, they indulged them too much. And in doing this, they robbed them of the "healthy hunger" that would eventually drive them to acquire for themselves.

"We Were Afraid Our Kids Wouldn't Like Us"

A terribly destructive notion that has arisen among modern parents is the idea that they should be their child's friend, that they must stay in their child's good graces at all times, and at all costs. They are terrified of their children's disapproval, and God forbid, their wrath.

Aside from fear, I see that a good bit of this mistaken notion arises from the parents' guilt at not spending more time with their children. They try to appease their child and make up for the lost time by lavishing gifts upon them.

Children do need to share a bond of affection with their parents, of course. But if their own parents abdicate the tasks of discipline and guidance in order to win a popularity contest, who then will guide them through the less pleasant lessons life has to offer? For, as luck would have it, these are the very experiences that flex our children's character-muscles. Without developing the strength to conquer adversity, their capacity for true joy will remain pitifully small.

"We Were Just Trying to Give Them a Great Childhood"

This cycle is devastatingly easy to fall into. We give our kids the things we would have loved when we were young. We share their joy vicariously—it's almost as if we're getting a second shot at childhood. But then we think, if this much brings them happiness, won't a little more make them even happier?

Yet for some reason, the more we give, the less happiness it seems to bring them. Have you ever noticed that second helpings never taste as good as the first? That rush of excitement over buying a new car, TV or DVD player never lasts long. Recall the disappointment you felt after you realized that the new house, boat, or raise didn't give you the pleasure you'd hoped for. How many times have you stopped to realize that having more and more means less and less?

When our kids respond to our gifts, not with happy gratitude, but with a petulant demand for more, our joyful gift-giving turns into appeasement. But a bigger dose of the wrong medicine will never cure the patient.

"Why Burden Our Kids With Financial Matters?"

An old saying warns us, "Credit is what keeps you from knowing how far past broke you are." Many affluent parents fall prey to what Thomas Stanley and William Danko refer to as "economic outpatient care": they automatically foot the bill for their children's extravagant lifestyle. This encourages them to expect a lifestyle they can neither sustain nor maintain on their own. When parents open the tap on a never-ending stream of cash, children see no particular reason to learn to regulate the flow.

Compounding the problem is a notion prevalent among the upper class that financial matters as an inappropriate topic for conversation. I've had clients who would sooner tell me their darkest sexual depravities than discuss their financial bottom line. Money is considered a particularly taboo subject to discuss with children.

"They shouldn't have to worry about that kind of thing at their age," one mother argued.

But the longer we wait to begin their financial education, the greater the risk we run that they will never learn to manage money sensibly.

No matter how much we shell out for them, they're the ones who pay the greatest price for their ignorance. Their financial dependence on us robs them of a sense of their own self-sufficiency. Devoid of a sense of capable independence, how happy can they ever be?

"We've Told Them Money Isn't Everything"

"Do as I say, not as I do"—what child ever bought into that old dicitm? Actions always speak louder than words, yet parents often preach one set of values and model another. It's easier to push water uphill than to train a child in a way that the parents don't go themselves.

If you keep telling them to value people for their character and their achievements, not for their material wealth, but they're forever observing you "keeping up with the Joneses," you're never going to win that battle.

It is always harder to cleave to your values than to give in to temptations. And of course, we all fall short of perfection some of the time. But if we don't show them that it can be done, where are they going to learn it?

Children who learn to equate self-worth with net worth are far from happy. They are left to live out their lives with the nagging fear that without their fortunes, they'd be nothing.

What We Really Want for Our Children

At this point, there should be no doubt in our minds that money can't buy our children's happiness. Realizing that a sense of well-being is largely independent of being well off is a liberating notion. It frees us from feeling like we have to buy two thousand dollar suits, expensive homes or luxury cars, all in the elusive pursuit of happiness. It liberates us from envying the lifestyles of the rich and famous, killing ourselves to build fortunes in a vain effort to assure our children's welfare. Best of all, it releases us to invest ourselves in developing the traits, attitudes, activities and atmosphere that will promote our own, and ultimately our children's, well being—the very things that pave the way for *true* happiness.

The Secret to Happiness: It's All In Your Head

If money can't really buy happiness, how can we ever be happy with money? The University of Michigan's national surveys may shed some light on this question. They determined that what mattered more than a person's actual wealth was their perceived wealth.

Put simply, *our happiness resides more in our heads than in our wallets.*

Money itself is at least two steps removed from happiness. It's not the size of our income that makes us happy, it's how satisfied we are with the income we have. If we're content with our net worth, regardless of the amount, we're more likely to say that we're happy. *Happiness is not so much getting what you want as wanting what you have.*

Seneca observed this fact over two thousand years ago: "Our forefathers…lived every jot as well as we, when they provided and dressed their own meat with their own hands, lodged upon the ground and were not as yet come to the vanity of gold and gems…which may serve to show us that it is the mind, and not the sum, which makes any person rich…No one can be poor that has enough, nor rich, that covets more than he has."

To be rich and happy is to have wants that are simpler than our incomes can afford. Even John D. Rockefeller, one of the world's wealthiest men, realized this truth, and constantly tried to simplify his life by reducing his wants. "If a man feels rich on ten dollars, he was fond of saying, "and has everything else he desires, he is really rich."

This gives us two ways to be rich, but only one way to be happy. To be wealthy, we may either possess great riches, or we may be content with what we have. But only the latter generates happiness.

Moreover, our income level doesn't noticeably affect the satisfaction we have with friendships, marriage, family, or ourselves—all the things that *do* reliably predict our degree of happiness. Amazing as it may seem, if they're not wracked by hunger or hurt, people of all degrees of prosperity enjoy comparable levels of joy and contentment.

We sometimes mistakenly pity the poor, thinking only of their financial hardship, while losing sight of what theologian Gustavo Gutierrez observed of the Third World, "The believing poor have never lost their capacity for having a good time and celebrating, despite the harsh conditions in which they live."

Just as it's possible to be rich and miserable, it's also possible to be poor and pleased.

Psychologist Ed Deiner and his colleagues at the University of Illinois found that four out of five of the people they surveyed, all with net worths well over $100 million, agreed that "money can increase or decrease happiness, depending on how it's used."

And quite a few were unhappy indeed. One tremendously wealthy man in the survey said he could never remember being happy. One woman reported that money could not repair all the misery caused by her children's problems. Another highly successful real estate agent in her late fifties, with two painful divorces in her past, lamented, "No matter what I've gained in life, I've never felt that anyone ever loved me for the person I am."

To be happy, then, requires an adjustment to our thinking, not our net worth. If we wish our children to be truly happy, this is the most important lesson we must pass on to them.

Helping Your Children Grow Healthy, Wealthy and Wise

What are these traits, attitudes, activities and atmospheres that help your child attain genuine happiness? Let's look at each in turn:

Healthy: One of my favorite definitions of emotional health describes it as *an ongoing commitment to reality at all costs.* Along with this undying commitment to deal with life as it is, a healthy individual needs to have confidence in their place in it, and in their ability to handle it effectively. This is where self-esteem comes in.

Self-esteem is not the same thing as self-love, which tends to put people in mind of arrogance and conceit. The egotism and narcissistic selfishness that we associate with these traits are actually due to a *lack* of self-esteem. People who truly feel good about themselves have no need to prop up their egos. True self-esteem allows us to love ourselves for who we are, which in turn makes it possible for us to love others. Psychologist Nathaniel Brandon tells us that our love of ourselves is directly related to our capacity to love others: "...the higher the level of self-esteem, the more likely one will treat others with respect, kindness and generosity."

Self-esteem is made up of three core components: self-respect, assertiveness, and self-efficacy. Self-respect is our belief in our own value. It has no need to compare itself with others, as egotism does, for it is confident of its own intrinsic worth. Assertiveness allows us to honor and appropriately express our needs, wants and feelings. It is different from aggression, which gratifies needs at the expense of others. Self-efficacy is our belief in our own competence. With this trait in place, we are confident in our ability to handle whatever challenges life may throw at us.

If one of these three factors is missing, the equation doesn't work. The Spooners' lifestyle hampers the development of all three. The exaggerated emphasis on material worth may lead them to think of their own worth in terms of dollar signs. Of what value then, would they be without their fat bankroll? The Spooners' classic lack of motivation saps their capacity for assertiveness. The pampering and sheltering that Spooners receive from parents, servants, nannies, trust officers and others rob them of the chance to develop the confidence they need to prove their own efficacy to themselves. Add to this the fact that Spooners typically go through childhood without adequate nurturing or guidance, and it becomes easy to see why Spooners doubt their own lovability, worth, and effectiveness in dealing with the world.

Wealthy: We've discussed the fact that wealth offers diminishing returns after a point. How much money, then, does a person need in order to enjoy the benefits of true wealth before enough becomes too much? I believe that a person is truly wealthy when they have enough money to maintain their lifestyle without having to work—though ideally they would still choose to do so. Wealth so defined can be a tremendous liberator. Free from financial worry, individuals who are wealthy by this definition are able to concentrate all their energies on their life's work and on the people and things they love.

But as I'm sure you can see, wealth is far more a matter of attitude than of dollars. Even if you plan to leave your kids wealthy—something I discourage in a later chapter—children must learn to appropriately value and handle money. If they do not, there is no fortune in the world so large that it cannot be squandered. For children to be prosperous on their own, they must learn to respect and manage money—and have a reason to work for it. Wealth comes as a result of a strong work ethic; it *remains* as a result of sound money-handling practices.

Wise: In my mind, and in the minds of many parents, wisdom is the measure of how well a person manages in the world. Wisdom is not knowledge accumulation. It doesn't come from a high degree of formal education—-many bright, well-educated people are failures in life. Wise people are smart, not purely in an intellectual sense, but in the way that they are able to keep their heads even in the most challenging circumstances.

Daniel Goleman, author of the best-selling book *Emotional Intelligence*, reveals the true meaning of intelligence as the ability to fare well in life. He argues that the capacity for self-control, zeal, persistence, and self-motivation, what is collectively referred to as emotional intelligence, plays a more significant role in our lives than does traditional IQ. The ability to motivate oneself and persist in the face of setbacks, to consciously change our feelings and moods, to control impulses and postpone gratification, to keep stress from swamping our ability to concentrate, to relate well with others—these are the traits that define true wisdom. It is precisely these emotional competencies that ultimately determine our success in life, material and otherwise.

Parents often lose sight of this fact. They get caught up in the frenzy of getting their kids into the top schools and pressuring them to make the best grades, believing that this is a sure ticket to prosperity. Parents, particularly if they are high achievers, mistakenly conclude that if they push their children to top out their academic performance, that this will assure them the best jobs and highest salaries. Yet studies have shown that at best, IQ contributes only about 20% to the factors that determine success in life—about the same as luck.

Certainly we want our kids to go to good schools, do well academically, and land great jobs. But unfortunately in the process we often take our eyes off the real prize: *the way they're developing emotionally and psychologically*. This is what determines their ultimate success in the world. How adept a person is in the "soft" skills—emotional control, stress tolerance, integrity, people skills—explains why some high-achievers thrive and others of equal or superior intellect fail.

Let's look at the role of just one of these emotional competencies, positive motivation: the ability to generate feelings of excitement, enthusiasm and confidence in achieving difficult goals. When you examine the highly successful, the best of the best, no matter what their pursuit, whether they be chess grand masters, CEOs, elite athletes or world class musicians, what you find is their unifying ability to motivate themselves to pursue their craft. Don't think for a moment that these achievers didn't get discouraged, tired, frustrated, bored, or disgusted. They surely suffered moments when the easiest choice would have been to throw in the towel. They learned to resist the impulse to quit. They denied the urge to cash in, and stayed the course no matter what. This ability to pursue goal-directed delayed gratification is the cornerstone of self-discipline and emotional maturity, yet it is but one facet of the intangible attribute we call wisdom.

These, then, are the things we *really* want for our kids when we say we want them to be happy. Parents, no matter what their net worth, want their children to be emotionally and physically sound, financially secure, and adept at handling the realities of life. But in the mad scramble for financial gain, they lose sight of the fact that none of these attributes can be bought.

Parents can't *give* these traits to their children at all. Ambition, self-control, reciprocity, responsibility and sensible values—the antitheses of the Silver Spooner Syndrome—cannot be given, only earned. Children must go after these things themselves, or they will never achieve them.

All we parents can do is clear the path. And lovingly, firmly, consistently guide them in the right direction. But they must be the ones to make the journey.

When we shower them with material goods, we literally clutter their route to maturity. We clog the works. And when we further compound this logjam by being unavailable to them so much of the time, we cannot do an adequate job of guiding their steps or bolstering their confidence.

If you've made some mistakes—and we all have—don't despair. *All* of these unhealthy behaviors are 100% learned. If your children could learn them in the first place, they can unlearn them. For the balance of this book, you'll receive a proven prescription for helping your children unlearn the harmful habits that are choking them.

Even if your children have reached young adulthood, it's never too late to see positive results. In general, the younger the child, the more effective the prescriptions in this book will be—although in my clinical practice, I've seen these techniques help "kids" in their thirties and forties to come around.

But we must act as early as we can. Once our kids pass the age of twelve, studies indicate that external forces quickly outstrip the parents' influence. By the time children enter middle adulthood in their mid-thirties, they are becoming set in their ways, and attitudes and behaviors become extremely difficult to alter. The younger our children, the better the odds of reversing the paralyzing effects of the Silver Spoon Syndrome.

Chapter Three:

The Rescue Plan:
Curing the Plague of Prosperity

*Will you tell me how to prevent luxury from producing
effeminacy, intoxication, extravagance, vice and folly?*
—John Adams

In this chapter I'll introduce you to a powerful paradigm that breaks the destructive cycle of the Silver Spoon Syndrome and builds the foundation for healthy self-esteem, ambition, self-control, and wisdom. I've developed this program over the course of two decades in order to help the children of my clients. Its success rate is outstanding.

Once we've discussed the paradigm in detail, I'll offer you a series of hands-on, prescriptive "anti-spoiling" exercises aimed at curing your child of the dreaded Silver Spoon Syndrome. But first I must make one thing perfectly clear: if this remedy is to have any meaningful effect whatsoever, it must begin with a change of attitude.

Not your child's attitude. Yours.

911 for Spooners in Peril: Practicing the 5 Life-Salvaging Laws

As you implement this rescue plan, you'll be putting into practice the Five Immutable Laws of Financial Parenting, which together make up an unstoppable paradigm that lights a fire under the unmotivated, promotes emotional resilience, stops greed in its tracks, blazes a trail for fiscal responsibility, and restores a healthy balance of financial values. Think of these not so much in the legal sense, but more as "natural laws," akin to the laws of electricity or thermodynamics. These five potent, undeniable forces can wreak havoc in the lives of those who do not respect them. But when we learn to properly harness their energy, they will propel us, and our children, toward true emotional and financial health.

I'll warn you now, if you haven't seen it coming already: you may recognize yourself in these laws. Our children's dysfunctional behavior developed largely in response to their environment, which we, as parents, helped to create for them. Before we can expect a change in their behavior, we must take a long, hard, unflinching look at our own, and mend it where we can. That's the real secret to harnessing the Five Laws.

#1: The Law of Necessity

Children develop a healthy motivational drive when desire compels them into action. They can only develop ambition through the act of pursuing the things they want. Parents have a duty to provide their children with necessities, but it's also their duty *not* to provide too many *non*-necessities. When children receive effortlessly whatever they desire, their natural motivational impulses are dampened, if not destroyed. Parents must give children the opportunity to want something badly enough to go after it themselves. **DON'T give them more material comfort than they absolutely need!**

#2: The Law of Loving Limits

Material wealth can *never* replace firm, loving parenting. Children need to have their parents care for them and set appropriate limits on their behavior. They need to be told what is acceptable and what's not. They must be taught to treat others with respect. They must learn to understand that they cannot always have things their way. In order to mature emotionally, children need to know their limits. **DO fulfill these nonmaterial needs—especially their need for "no."**

#3: The Law of Reciprocity

In order to develop a balanced sense of their place in the world, children must learn the dynamics of give and take. Narcissistic entitlement occurs when children remain forever on the receiving end without being expected to give in return. When parents teach their children to *earn* the things they receive, and to appreciate what they have, they help them to avoid developing a sense of entitlement. **DO insist that they earn what they receive.**

#4: The Law of Fiscal Responsibility

Children cannot develop a healthy relationship to money unless they learn to handle it properly. Parents must teach their children the basics of money management, lest the children grow up thinking of money as an endlessly renewable resource. **DO teach them money management!**

#5: The Law of Example

Children gain their first and most enduring set of values by observing their parents. If their parents judge others by what they have instead of who they are, they may grow up to confuse self-worth with net worth. If they see their parents spending money carelessly, they may think little of the effort required to earn it. If parents lecture their child about the appropriate value of money, but do not model that value in their own lives, their children may grow up with a distorted view of its importance. **DO practice what you preach!**

As you've no doubt guessed, each of the five core symptoms of the Silver Spoon Syndrome corresponds to one of the corrective Laws of Financial Parenting:

Corrective Laws of Financial Parenting

- **Persistent Underachievement = The Law of Necessity**
- **Low Frustration Tolerance = The Law of Loving Limits**
- **Narcissistic Entitlement = The Law of Reciprocity**
- **Fiscal Illiteracy = The Law of Fiscal Responsibility**
- **Distorted Values = The Law of Example**

The rescue plan upon which you're now embarking enables you to minister directly to each of the five areas. When we put the whole picture together, matching symptoms, characteristics and results together with their corresponding laws, diagnostic tests and prescriptive cures, this is what we get:

Symptom #1: Persistent Underachievement.
Usual Course: Ranges from adolescence to adulthood.
Characteristics: Boredom, listlessness, lack of direction, living for the moment.
Potential Results: Emotional, social and intellectual immaturity. Depression. Underachievement. Low self-esteem.
Test: Is Your Child Suffering from Persistent Underachievement?
Cause: Parents do everything for the child, depriving the child of the urge to do for him/herself.
Law: Law of Necessity: DON'T give them more material comforts than they need.
Prescription: Stoking an Appetite for Success.
Outcome: Children learn to set goals and go after the things they want.

Symptom #2: Low Frustration Tolerance.
Usual Course: Common and annoying in early childhood; a growing concern in adolescence, a serious problem in adulthood.
Characteristics: Tantrums, pouting, easily annoyed by obstacles, quit easily when faced with adversity, can't delay gratification.
Potential Results: Poor social skills, stress-related illnesses, substance abuse and a consistent pattern of work and relationship failures.
Test: Are You Giving Them "Things" When You Should Be Giving Them Discipline?
Cause: Parents fail to discipline children because they don't want to deal with the child's rage, for fear that the child will not like them, or out of guilt that they are not spending enough time with them. They give *things* instead of *themselves*. They give in to demands instead of setting limits on them.
Law: Law of Loving Limits: DO Fulfill Their Nonmaterial Needs— Including Their Need for "No."

Prescription: Turn Tantrums Into Emotional Resilience.
Outcome: Children learn to delay gratification, overcome frustration, and successfully accomplish long-term goals.

Symptom #3: Narcissistic Entitlement.
Usual Course: Common and normal in early childhood, most pronounced in Adolescence, pathological in adulthood.
Characteristics: The child expects things to come to them without effort on their part. Lack of empathy. Expects special treatment. Fantasies of unrealistic success. The child feels they have a right to status,power, and money by virtue of birth rather than honest achievement. Commonly called "spoiled."
Potential Results: Dissatisfaction, emptiness, underlying apprehension, isolation, depression. Shallow relationships.
Test: Do You Feed Their Greed?
Cause: Parents give without expecting anything in return.
Law: Law of Reciprocity: DO Make Them Earn What They Receive.
Prescription: Breaking the Back of Entitlement.
Outcome: Children learn give and take; they learn to respect the needs of others.

Symptom #4: Fiscal Illiteracy
Usual Course: More notable in adolescence and painfully obvious in adulthood.
Characteristics: Inability to manage money. "Easy come, easy go": excessive spending, poor consumer choices, bounced checks, over-extended credit, failure to pay bills, failure to live within means.
Potential Results: Destruction of credit and reputation, frequent requests for bail-outs, low self-esteem, financial dependency.
Test: Are You Teaching Your Child Money Management?
Cause: Parents failed to teach money management skills, excluded children from the family's financial life.
Law: Law of Fiscal Responsibility: DO Teach Them Money Management.
Prescription: Raising Your Child's Financial IQ.
Outcome: Children learn to handle money responsibly.

Symptom #5: Distorted Values.

Usual Course: Becomes more problematic in adolescence and adulthood.

Characteristics: Manifests at any age but becomes obvious by adolescence. Inappropriate emphasis on material possessions. The child's mood and self-esteem is tied to what they have rather than who they are.

Potential Results: The child may overvalue money, believing that it means *everything* (money can buy happiness, self-worth, etc.) or the child may *undervalue* money, believing that it means *nothing*, and spend it recklessly.

Test: Do You Practice What You Preach?

Cause: Parents do not model an appropriate relationship to money. They may say, "money isn't everything," yet act as if it is.

Law: Law of Example: DO Practice What You Preach.

Prescription: Model a Healthy Relationship to Money.

Outcome: Children learn to value money appropriately.

As you work your way through the remainder of the book, you'll find that each core symptom has a chapter of its own. In it, you'll find a diagnostic test that will help you determine how severe your child's problem is in that particular area. Then you'll move onto to a prescriptive exercise that will guide you through the "cure."

These prescriptions will help you to "brat-proof" your younger children, and will also help you to "un-spoil" the child who is already showing symptoms. Read through the entire chapter before you begin working the exercise. Make absolutely certain that you're committed to the full course of the prescription. If you make nothing more than a half-hearted attempt, or if your resolve fizzles before you've seen results, you run the risk of doing more harm than good.

Write out the Five Laws of Financial Parenting and post them someplace where you'll bump into them frequently. If you don't remain consistently invested in the principles they represent, you will not stay the course. You must believe passionately in what you're doing, because you are in for a struggle. It takes tremendous resolve to overcome inertia, to change inculcated patterns of behavior, to break comfortable-but-dangerous habits. Ask any overeater. Ask any smoker, drug addict or alcoholic. Your family's unhealthy addiction to material wealth is every bit as tough a nut to crack.

And worse yet, you'll have to brace yourself for the possibility that you'll be going it alone. You may actually be in for a lot of grief from relatives, friends, even your spouse, who may misunderstand your change of behavior toward your child. They may be unwilling to face their own dysfunctional relationships with money, and may see your efforts toward better financial health as an indictment against them. When they see you changing, they'll most likely put all kinds of pressure on you to change you back. They'll probably tell you you're being mean, selfish, stingy, arrogant and judgmental. They may even try to undermine your efforts. So you will have to hang tough, stick it out—deal with your opponents gently and firmly, but stay your course. Your child's future depends on it.

One Law to Rule Them All: The Law of Priorities

Before we plunge into the curative portion of the book, one last word of caution: the prescriptions in this book are very unlikely to help you or your child unless you are aware of the basic principle behind all of these laws:

**Our Children's Non-material *Needs*
ALWAYS Take Priority
Over Their, Or Our, Material *Wants***

We must keep this paradigm foremost in our thinking as we're shepherding our children through these exercises, for without it, the Five Laws are meaningless. We now know that the Silver Spoon Syndrome develops when parents shower their children with material indulgence instead of loving guidance. As much as they might tell you otherwise, our kids don't *need* a Playstation2. Or a new BMW. They DO need our love, our guidance, and our good example.

They will sustain no lasting damage from doing without the "stuff." But if they don't receive sufficient daily amounts of loving, involved parenting, they will eventually develop a debilitating "emotional malnutrition" that will wreak havoc with their ability to achieve true happiness. Sure, it's easier to slap down a credit card and indulge their latest whim. But it's our job to give them what they need, not what they want.

And we've seen where that's getting us. The longer we wait to change our unhealthy relationship to money, the more devastating it's likely to be for our children. Let's begin the transformation. Now.

PART TWO:

THE FIVE IMMUTABLE LAWS OF FINANCIAL PARENTING

Chapter Four:

Don't Give Them More Material Comfort Than They Need: The Law of Necessity

Luxury is more deadly than any foe.

—Juvenal

Parents often ask me, "Just how much can I help my kids financially without hurting them?" Affluent parents have a lot to give, which means they face this question every day. They worry that money will ruin their children, yet they feel compelled to let their kids enjoy the benefits of their wealth. But how do parents strike a healthy balance? How much is too much?

Look to your kids for the answer.

For parents, it's one of the most frightening symptoms of "rich kid's disease": the bored, listless, ambitionless child who drifts aimlessly through what ought to be the most passionate, ambitious years of his life. These kids have so much, their anguished parents tell me, yet they care for so little.

Do you suspect that your child is developing this symptom? Could your generosity, however well intentioned, be sapping your child's motivation? This test will provide some answers:

Self-Test: Is Your Child Suffering from "Persistent Underachievement"?

1. Does your child have trouble developing and pursuing goals and interests?
   Yes   No

2. Do you worry that your child doesn't seem to care about anything?
   Yes   No

3. Do you have to push your child to take care of responsibilities—school attendance, chores, studying, work?
   Yes   No

4. Do you worry that your children may never reach their full potential?   Yes   No

5. Do you find yourself doing things for your children that you know they can do for themselves?
   Yes   No

6. Do you buy nonessential things for your kids in order to protect them from the "discomfort" of doing without?
   Yes   No

7. When they complain of boredom, do you buy things to keep your children entertained, instead of encouraging them to develop interests?
   Yes   No

8. When they want a particular item, do you reflexively buy it for them instead of suggesting that they earn it—or do without it?
   Yes   No

9. Do you give your children gifts that "mindlessly entertain" (video games, electronic toys) more often than you give "nutritious" gifts that stimulate and develop their interests (board games, musical instruments, sports equipment, books)?
   Yes   No

10. Do you go overboard with presents at birthdays and holidays because you want your children to have a better childhood than you did?

   Yes   No

   For each Yes, score 1 point. For each No, score 0.

- If you scored from 0-3, consider yourself fortunate. Your children probably don't have any serious problems with their level of motivation—or at least, not ones you're creating.
- A score that falls between 4-8 suggests that your child is at risk for developing motivational problems. You and your child are facing some corrective work in the "ambition" department.
- Any score above 8 is definitely reason to worry. Scores at this level clearly indicate an amotivational syndrome. You will want to apply the prescription offered in this chapter first. If these problems persist, outside professional consultation may be needed.

If your child is falling into a pattern of underachievement, then you know it's time to cut back on their material comfort level. They need to feel the hunger of doing without to restart their motivational engines. But how do we set the right limits on our giving?

The Five Absolute Needs vs. Endless Wants: Teaching Kids the Difference

There's no question that more money brings more of the so-called "good things" in life: a Colorado condo, a trip to France, a new luxury car. Who wouldn't rather have a new BMW than a used Buick? Yet we have seen that all these fine things add little to our emotional bottom line, and that a glut of them can destroy our kids' motivation. When so much comes to them effortlessly, why should they exert themselves? It's as though we're serving them a sumptuous twelve-course banquet, day after day, then we wonder why they won't get up, go to the kitchen, and make themselves a turkey sandwich.

No one denies that we genuinely need a certain amount of money to avoid deprivation. Everyone needs food, rest, shelter, medical care and human contact. But our legitimate needs don't end at mere creature comforts. Psychologist Abraham Maslow's Hierarchy of Needs illustrates that once our basic physical needs are met, other social and psychological needs, such as a sense of belonging and self-worth, come to the fore. We have as much of a responsibility to provide for our children in these nonmaterial areas as we do to provide them with adequate food and clothing. *But when we provide material comfort for them far beyond their basic needs, we block the means by which these nonmaterial needs are met!*

Once we have met our children's basic needs, providing financial support beyond that point is fraught with danger. The only true obligation parents have is to meet their child's basic material and emotional needs—and even this responsibility changes significantly as our kids hit age eighteen. Anything more a parent does is gravy. Remember, adult children are not *entitled* to anything!

In our abundant culture, it's ridiculously easy for kids to develop a "gotta have it" mentality. With store after store full of things to buy, with television shows built around merchandising, with clever advertisements everywhere that promise to solve all our problems and make us instantly, deliriously happy, kids are bombarded with things to want.

Parents have to be able to distinguish needs from wants—both our own, and our children's. In fact, if parents can't make this distinction in their own day-to-day decision-making, we can hardly expect them to teach their kids this critical distinction.

It's our job to teach them that wants come and go, that we will always have desires, and that if we live our lives in a perpetual frenzy of trying to fulfill our every whim, we will never know true satisfaction. In order to keep their sanity, children must develop the ability to recognize that spike of desire that can cause an impulse purchase. We must teach them that the irresistible longing they feel for a particular item, which seems all-consuming for weeks on end, will be forgotten this time next year—along with the object of their desire. And we must help them see that, in most cases, the *wanting* almost always turns out to be nicer than the *having.*

Kids—even adult children—often can't see the difference between wants and needs by themselves. To them, wanting is the same as needing. It's up to us to teach them, from an early age, that their bodies need food, water, clothing, medical attention and shelter, and that their minds and spirits need love, acceptance, discipline and guidance. But *no* part of them *needs* a BMW!

Rx #1: Stoking an Appetite for Success

Step #1: Start Them on a "Material Diet": Whenever indulgent parents ask me why their children lack motivation, I respond with an old truism: "Give me one good reason why kids would work for something when it's freely given."

The first thing we must do, then, if we want to spark a fire under unmotivated children, is to staunch the flow of nonessential items. We must stop giving them things they don't absolutely need.

I know you may cringe at the prospect of this. You may feel that you're being mean to them. And trust me, they'll probably respond as though you are! But you're actually doing them a kindness, exactly as you would be doing by denying doughnuts to an obese child. In fact, the older the child, the fewer non-essentials you should provide.

Sit down with your child and explain what you're doing, and why. The conversation might go something like this:

"Your mom and I have realized that we've been making a big mistake. We've been giving you lots of nice things because we wanted to make you happy. But we realize now that when we give you the things you want, we're robbing you of the experience of getting them for yourself. We've lost sight of the fact that you're growing up, and that what you really need us to do is to help you get ready for being an adult. We've been taking responsibility and independence *away from you*, rather than helping you gain it.

"So, starting today, we're going to make some changes. Of course, we'll still feed you and clothe you and give you a safe place to live. But all the extra stuff you want will be your responsibility. From now on, when there's something you want that's not a necessity, you'll have the opportunity to work for it yourself, the way adults do. If you like, we'll help you work out a plan for getting the stuff you want, and of course, whenever you feel that you need guidance, we'll be here. But from now on, we want you to find out how good it feels to earn things for yourself."

When you finish your announcement, don't expect smiles, hugs and applause. Do expect you're your child to be stunned, angry, and in disbelief. They'll be stunned that you'd even try it, angry because you're cutting off their goodies, and disbelieving, because they know your track record. In fact, they're already working on ways to get around the new "diet."

This change of policy will be difficult to accomplish if your spouse is not on board. If both parents aren't of one mind, your children will quickly learn to play one parent off against the other. Enlist the cooperation of other family members as well. It won't help much for you to cut off his tab at the country club if Aunt Petunia is going to cough up another $1,000 any time the kid makes Bambi eyes at her. Be firm: explain what you're trying to do, and graciously ask that they not undermine your efforts with lavish gifts or cash.

You may worry that you'll look like a villain to the rest of the family—and you might. Some might even gang up on you in a misguided rescue attempt. I can't guarantee that every person will appreciate the difficult, loving thing you're trying to do. But you must resolve to do this anyway, no matter what they think. The results will be worth it.

Step #2: Let Them "Suffer" for a While: It may be difficult for you to watch, but whatever you do, don't give in! Think of the message that would send them: "You're right, you *are* incapable of doing without." It may stomp all over your parental instincts at first, to leave your beloved offspring in such pain! But in truth, you're giving them a beautiful gift. They'll not only survive, they will grow from the experience. Keep in mind that discomfort is a necessary condition for curing this symptom. A little hardship is a necessary catalyst for success.

Step #3: Outline an Achievement Plan: Now that you've placed them in a hole, you're going to hand them the ladder, and let them climb their way out! Don't try to do this if they're still in "righteous anger" mode. Wait until they've gone "hungry" long enough that their appetite is beginning to waken. Wait until they've tested you and found that they can't crack your resolve.

When you start hearing things like, "You mean I can't *ever* have a BMX bike?" that's your cue. You can respond with something like, "Yes, there is a way you can get that bike. You can *earn* it. I'll help you work out a way to do that."

Have them choose a moderately priced item that they want. Start small at first, so that they can get a taste of success. Then help them work out a plan for earning it. Each subsequent goal you set can raise the stakes a bit.

Make sure that the goal is age-appropriate: if you agree to let your 12-year-old rake leaves to earn money for a Mitsubishi Diablo, you're setting him up to fail! But a 17-year-old is going to need a more challenging goal than the latest Britney Spears CD, which she can buy after cashiering for only a single day at Bloomingdale's.

Give your children the task of researching the cost of the item. Then have them work out a plan for raising the necessary cash. Have them do the math: if they can earn $40 flipping burgers each weekend, how many weeks will it take them to earn the amount they'll need to buy that quadraphonic stereo? Mark the date on a calendar. Have them pencil in the amount they've earned and saved at the end of each week.

With older adolescents, you may want to choose an ongoing expense such as a monthly cell phone bill or car insurance. Set a cut-off date: "I'll cover you until March 1st when your policy comes up for renewal. By that time you've either got to be making that $150 a month yourself, *consistently*, or you're handing over the keys."

With young adults 18 years or older, the issue may go beyond mere luxuries. Are they still hanging around at home, without any clear goals for moving out on their own? When your children reach this age, you not only don't owe them "the finer things," you don't even owe them the basic necessities! The goals you set at this stage should be oriented toward getting them out on their own: get them accustomed to paying rent and utilities, help them set up a monthly budget for food, gas and other necessities, and set a "move out date" by which time they'll need to have secured a new place to live. For more tips on getting these late bloomers out of the house, see the section in Chapter Ten entitled, "Emptying the Nest: Launching the Reluctant Teenager."

Whatever their age, reassure your kids that you have confidence in them, be sympathetic if they need to talk, but *don't* do the work for them! Let them experience the consequences of their own actions.

Step #4: Check Their Progress Regularly: Just like any good coach would, make this a joint effort between yourself and your child. As they make the transition, sit down regularly for an open, frank discussion. Are your kids making a decent effort? Are they "on target" for success? Are you seeing an improvement in their attitudes? Don't lecture or cajole. Just listen and discuss.

If they're doing well, *DON'T* give in to the temptation to reward them with "stuff." *DON'T* "help" them achieve their payoff early just because they're doing a good job, and *DON'T* reward a partial effort—after all, the real world never does. These may seem obvious to most of you, but you'd be surprised at how many parents succumb to the temptation to slip back into old habits.

DO encourage and praise their positive steps toward their goals. DO offer concrete guidance and advice—but only if it's asked for. DO express confidence in their ability to accomplish their goals for themselves.

If they're putting in the effort but not getting the results you hoped for, it's time to pinpoint the trouble spot. They may be plenty willing, but deficient in some critical skills. Are they having trouble finding employment? They may need help with the basics of job-searching and interviewing. Are they making too little money to meet the goal in time? Discuss the steps it will take to find higher-paying employment. Is it possible that the time frame you chose is unrealistic? You may need to revise it—but only after they've made an effective case for change.

If they're digging in their heels, check yourself: If you're seeing no improvement at all in their motivation level or their attitude, you might still be providing them with too fat a cushion. You may need to strip down their lifestyle even further in order to "starve them out." A little bit of deprivation—if we can even call it that—never hurt anyone.

But if you've pared them down to a mattress on the floor and two changes of clothes, and they're *still* mad as hell and refusing to make any effort to better themselves, you may have to call in the big guns. Consider an age-appropriate "shock therapy." I've advised a number of my clients to send their kids off to a boot camp, put them through a wilderness survival course or, if they're in their late teens or older, sign them up for a community service project that will bring them face to face with impoverished, at-risk inner city kids. This is very effective. Trust me, no matter how lean you've made their living conditions at home, it can't compare to the shock of what awaits them on an experience like this!

Step #5: Stay the Course: This program is very unlikely to work over the long haul unless you model the behavior you want to see in them. Your commitment to their progress must be ironclad. If they try to manipulate you, simply tell them, "I understand how you feel, but we're sticking to the program."

Success breeds success. Once their first small goals are achieved, encourage them to aim for bigger ones. Now that they have a few success stories of their own, they'll be better able to appreciate the struggles you went through to get where you are today. Their sense of confidence will improve, and they'll want to take on bigger challenges. With your guidance, your kids will be able to apply these motivational lessons to the bigger picture, because these same principles are the ones they'll use to build success throughout their adult lives.

Step #6: Cut 'Em Loose: At some point, you'll be convinced that they've mastered the basics of achievement and are moving in the right direction. A time will come when they have a string of successes under their belt. Your external prodding is now transforming into their own internal drive. Now, they'll seek out new challenges without your prompting. You'll be convinced that they've acquired the drive they need *and* the skills to go with it. This will be the time to quietly ease yourself out of the equation. Let them sink or swim on their own efforts!

Chapter Five:

Do Fulfill Their Non-Material Needs:
The Law of Loving Limits

When there is too much, something is missing.
—Leo Rosten

In the last chapter, we explored the idea that at times, parents give the most to their kids by *not* giving. We discovered that ambition actually requires a bit of deprivation in order to grow. Now, let's focus on the two most important nonmaterial gifts we can give our children: love, and limits.

Most parents find it easier to hug and kiss their children than to deny them. Limits are the harder side of love.

Do you have trouble telling your kids "no"? Do you cringe at the idea of having to set limits, for fear of damaging your child's tender psyche? Do you indulge your kids to make up for the time you're not spending with them? Does a creeping sensation of guilt keep you from reining in your child's behavior, even when you know you should? If so, you may be hampering your child's ability to tolerate frustration, a skill which will prove crucial to their success later in life.

If you suspect that your child has a low "no" tolerance, take the following test:

Self-Test: Are You Giving Them Things When You Should Be Giving Them Discipline?

1. Do your kids throw a tantrum when they don't get their way?
    Yes   No
2. Do your children give up too easily when faced with adversity?
    Yes   No
3. Does your child have a difficult time delaying gratification?
    Yes   No
4. Do you worry that your children's lack of self-control will hinder the development of their social skills?
    Yes   No
5. Do you cringe when you have to say "no" to your child?
    Yes   No
6. Do your children wear you down with persistent whining or pouting until you give in to their demands?
    Yes   No
7. Do you quickly give in, simply to avoid the bickering?
    Yes   No
8. Have you ever given your children gifts because you feel guilty for not spending enough time with them?
    Yes   No
9. Do you try to be your children's friend—when they need to you to be a parent?
    Yes   No
10. Do you worry that your kids won't like you?
    Yes   No

For each Yes, score 1 point. For each No, score 0.
- A score of 2 or less suggests, at most, a minor problem that will likely correct itself with time—and with firm, consistent limit-setting.
- A score that falls between 4-8 is reason for concern. If your child's older than 4 and still exhibiting these annoying behaviors, read this next section carefully and follow the prescriptions.

- A score above 8 suggests real problems, and the older the child, the more worried you should be. If these prescriptions don't clear up the problem, you may want to get professional consultation.

Platinum Hugs, Golden No's: The Two Keys to Raising Stronger Kids

It is tempting to take the easy way out and give things instead of ourselves. When we're busy, when the frantic minutia of life is pulling us in a thousand different directions, we look for shortcuts. It is easier to lavish children with stuff so that we can go about our important schedules. On the surface, it seems to work out fine: we get to pursue our work and social activities and the kids are distracted for a while with their new computers, dolls, Game Boys, televisions or BMWs. So where's the real harm?

It may not appear obvious to some, but kids need time with their parents. They must feel that they are important and loved unconditionally in order to have a chance to develop healthy self-esteem. We all want to give our kids the best in life, but we need to remember that "the best" goes far beyond the tangibles into the realm of love and nurturing.

All the expensive toys, cars, and exotic vacations in the world can't replace a child's feeling of being loved by their parents. Making them feel loved requires our time and energy, not our cash. Children need attention, affection, time, guidance, space, and safe places where they can learn and feel secure. They need play, touching, jokes, conversation, and unconditional caring. They need adults to set a good example. Without these, even the richest parents become the poorest parents.

Nurturing also involves doing things kids don't like. The harder part of love for many parents is setting limits, establishing boundaries, and giving our kids regular doses of the "No Vitamin." It's hard for wealthy parents to say no because they don't have to. They can afford to give their children whatever they wish. They give things and money because they can, not because they believe it's best for the child.

I've met many loving parents over the years that have the hardest time saying the simple word no to their children. They give in because they're afraid that their kids won't like them, because they worry that their children will throw a tantrum, or because they nurture a guilty belief that they are obligated to satisfy every whim. Some parents actually worry that their child will somehow be permanently scarred by the experience of frustration if they don't get their way. Nothing could be further from the truth. *These parents damage their children far more by neglecting their need for sensible limits.*

Kids need "No" to grow.

When They Ask for "Stuff," Give Them What Really Counts

It's natural to want to make your children happy, and to protect them from harm and pain. But that instinct, if not balanced, comes with a price: *children can't learn to become emotionally resilient if they don't get regular practice handling failure and frustration!*

It's certainly better for children to tackle their first experiences with frustration while they're still in the family's protective cocoon. But even parents of young adults can help their kids attain independence through the art of "supportive refusal." I've known plenty of parents who said no to their young adult children's demands for financial bailouts. They could have easily done what some would consider the loving thing: just fork over the cash! But they chose the more difficult path: they lovingly refused to cater to their adult children's dependency, and left them to solve their own troubles.

Their children floundered. But in the end, they found a way to solve their own problems.

When kids grow up in a blissful state of premature affluence, they often have trouble making the leap to independence. They often doubt their own untested resilience and resourcefulness. But when they are thrust into a sink or swim situation, they discover to their delight that they can make it!

I would argue that by saying no and allowing these young adults to work out their financial (and other) problems on their own, these parents demonstrated ultimate act of caring—an act that took great courage and foresight.

John D. Rockefeller, one of the world's wealthiest individuals, noted the value of adversity in shaping character: "Oh how blessed the young men are who have to struggle for a foundation and a beginning in life. I shall never cease to be grateful for the three and a half years of apprenticeship and the difficulties to be overcome, all the ways along."

John D. knew limits for the true gifts they are.

He also worked daily at passing his hard-earned character lessons along to his children, a task which we modern parents too often neglect. This generation of parents has done a wonderful job of sharing their standard of living with their kids, but a lousy job of providing them with the psychological and practical skills they need to achieve this same standard on their own. In short, we've made our children's lives too easy. We've created an unrealistic fantasy of the way the world works.

We've given too much and required too little.

Building for Success: How Resilience Makes All the Difference

If the purpose of raising kids is to help them learn to live lives of their own, parents have an obligation to train them for the real world, to give them experiences that will prepare them to survive on their own. Whether we like it or not, adult reality is filled with frustrations.

Through experience with obstacles, children learn to tolerate frustration. They learn to turn adversity into challenge, and persevere in the face of it. This ability to "hang in" when the going gets tough is a pillar of self-esteem and the primary quality in every success story, whether the endeavor is social, occupational, recreational, marital, or parental.

But if children are to encounter healthy doses of character-building frustration, parents must stop protecting their children from the consequences of their choices, and allow them to savor the bittersweet taste of reality. Parents must stop feeling guilty and charge ahead, staying focused on teaching their values no matter how their children respond. Because if you're saying no to an unreasonable demand, your child is going to be unhappy. In fact, on those occasions, their unhappiness tells you that you're on track!

Parents don't like to make their kids unhappy. Mistakenly, they believe that if the child is unhappy, they must be doing something wrong. Nothing could be further from the truth. Unhappiness, frustration, disappointment, anger, sadness are all part of life. The sooner we can teach our kids how to work through these feelings constructively, the stronger they become. A certain amount of unhappiness is essential to healthy character development and emotional growth.

As parents, we have to stand up to the pressures to give too much, whether that pressure comes from our children or from Madison Avenue.

This is the true test of love.

Rx #2: Turning Tantrums Into Emotional Resilience

Step # 1: Meet Professor No

There's no way around it: kids need you to give them limits. When their demands are excessive, or their behavior is unreasonable, put a stop to it. Whether your kids are three or forty-three, they cannot be healthy or at peace unless they learn when and how to rein in their own behavior.

Say no—and mean it.

The older your kids are, the harder they will fight you on this. If your kids are into their teens, brace yourself for all kinds of emotional pyrotechnics. Do explain to your older kids what has changed and why. Tell them that you've been remiss in this area of parenting, but that you're now going to correct your mistake.

They *will* fight you. They will test you in all kinds of interesting ways. But deep within their psyches, they'll be thanking you for it. They won't be consciously aware of it, but they've been dying for you to rein them in. They know they need it.

You're giving them a precious gift. Just don't expect a lot of gratitude—at least, not right off.

Step #2: Coaching Stick-To-It-Ness

Establish a "no quitters" rule. Tell your kids something like, "From now on I want you to really give some thought before you start something new, because once you start, I'm going to expect you to finish it."

Then when they hit the wall, be firm: "I know you're bored and frustrated, but you're going to finish these dance lessons. I'll help if I can but it's up to you to make something of the situation you choose." By keeping them in the situation, the child's forced to take full responsibility for their choice while also being given the opportunity to become creative and develop new strategies for dealing with difficult spots.

Good coaching may also take the form of praise, reassuring and encouraging words, and if asked, concrete advice. Be sure to reinforce the learning in the experience and not so much the outcome. Praise the little steps and mini-accomplishments toward the final goal. If Charlie trained daily for six months for a school track meet, gives it his all, and ends up in 6th place, help him feel good about his effort.

Another way to help them resist this impulse to quit, to deny the urge to cash in, to stay the course, is to get them to "buy in" on things they want. Encourage them to put some of their own hard-earned money, into the activity. Whether we're talking about dance lessons or college, kids are more likely to stick with things when it's their own dollars on the line.

Step # 3: Nudge, Guide, And Brush

As your kids become better able to set, pursue, and complete simple goals, nudge them to stretch themselves a little further. You can only nudge effectively if you're involved in their activities. Show up, get involved, be there to support them in what they're doing, whether it be the Boy Scouts, calculus, soccer, or playing the guitar. Your continued involvement here is critical.

Nudging *doesn't* mean shoving them into anything to occupy their time and get them off your back. The idea is to engage them in activities that encourage setting and achieving long-range objectives, to see that small consistent effort over time yields big results and satisfaction.

Be sure to encourage your kids to take chances. Guide them to try new things. Encourage them to venture outside of their comfort zone, and to risk the possibility of failure. You may need to brush them off after the fall, but be sure to let them get up on their own. Most importantly, help them to hang in there and sustain the effort even as the going gets tough. Don't let them give up, buy their way out, or just move on when things get difficult. Remember, they have to build their tolerance for failure in order to ever have a chance for success.

Step #4: When All Else Fails

The earlier steps will work for most children, but some parents start late, after the damage of permissiveness has gone on for years. For those adult children already seriously infected with the affluenza bug, there's still time for remedial work. If your older child still lives impulsively and recklessly and refuses to grow up, take action to eliminate any extra cushioning you're still providing. Even though you can't rescue them from themselves, you can opt not to financially support their destructive choices. You can only hope that sooner or later they'll "bottom out," which is where the real learning truly begins.

Before you end the dole, carefully explain yourself: "Jerry, I've done you an injustice by providing so much materially. It's kept you from truly experiencing the world. It's time I got out of your way financially. But I'll still be here for you emotionally."

Then brace yourself for the storm. I've seen these overgrown kids become righteously indignant when their parents turn off the cash flow. Occasionally, they'll yell and scream, cut off contact, refuse to let you see your grandkids, threaten suicide, or beg for reprieves in hopes that their parents will give in. Don't. If your relationship with your adult children is truly based on what you give them, then what exactly are you losing? You're actually doing both of you a favor by taking the money factor out of the relationship. But don't expect thanks. Just stand firm. Trust me, it will get better, but it will take time, as well as some discomfort on both sides.

Chapter Six:

Do Make Them Earn It:
The Law of Reciprocity

Up until the age of twelve, I sincerely believed
that everybody had a house on Fifth Avenue,
a villa in Newport and a steam-driven
ocean-going yacht.

—Cornelius Vanderbuilt, Jr.

Enough's Enough: No More "The World Owes Me" Attitudes

A child's life is largely determined by just how hard his mother and father work at being parents, the most difficult of all jobs. Parenting is so challenging because we learn how to do it *while we're doing it:* we first have to figure out what's best for our kids, then we must figure out how to give it to them. When you think of doing something that difficult, consistently, over a forty or fifty-year time span, it's no wonder we make mistakes! Parenthood is a journey of discovery where you overreact, improvise, and over time figure out what works. With any luck, over time, you improve.

Among all the other difficulties of parenthood, we all face the challenge of making sound decisions based on our child's needs and not our own. When we're tired, frustrated, harried, or hurting, it's easy to fall prey to the temptation to appease rather than parent.

As we discussed in the last chapter, it's much easier to give in to kids' wants than to put up with their whining, complaining, threats, and tantrums. When we do this, we rob our children of the opportunity to handle frustration, which keeps them from developing emotional resilience.

But low frustration tolerance is only one of the psychological goblins that plague overindulged children.

Meet Susie, the nine-year-old daughter of my client, Jane. Jane confessed to me that she brought home a toy to her daughter every day so that she would not have to face one of Susie's screaming fits. Jane was petrified that if she denied her child's wants, Susie would hate her. It's hard to say no to your child if your primary goal is to be liked.

Did Jane's daily purchases make Susie love her?

Not only did Susie refuse to show her mother much love, she never seemed satisfied with her daily acquisition. It had to be bigger, newer, better than the day before, or it was no good. Susie acted as though a daily toy was her God-given right. In fact, Susie hardly seemed to care about anything, or anyone, outside her own ever-escalating desire for more stuff.

"She has no use for me, except to demand more things," Jane wept bitterly.

Looking at Jane's mistake from the outside, it might be difficult for us to imagine how a parent could make such a glaring error. But the story becomes clearer when we understand that Jane habitually bought her daughter's love as a means of trying to fill her own emotional void. Like many love buyers, her own childhood had been marked more by money than affection. The fears that drive us to make foolish parenting choices are very often rooted in early childhood.

In my years as a therapist counseling the prosperous, I've met hundreds of people just like Jane who were still fleeing their own inner money-demons. They are the children of people who used their wealth to erect barricades to protect themselves, to stave off their inner fears of abandonment, to control and punish those around them, or to fund a desperate search for love and happiness. Many of these parents also came from families contaminated by these same issues. They can escalate as they're passed down from generation to generation.

Narcissistic entitlement, the trait that lonely, frightened love-buying Jane unwittingly fostered in her daughter Susie, is perhaps the most easily recognizable symptom of the Silver Spoon Syndrome. The following test will reveal whether or not this obnoxious characteristic is plaguing your child:

Self-Test: Do You Feed Their Greed?

1. Have you ever caught yourself thinking that your kids are "spoiled?"
   Yes   No

2. Do your children act as though you owe them the things they want?
   Yes   No

3. Do you feel that your children don't appreciate the things you give them?
   Yes   No

4. Does it seem that no matter how much you give, they act as though it's not enough?
   Yes   No

5. Does your child appear to be selfish, self-centered, or lacking empathy toward others?
   Yes   No

6. Do your children believe that they are better than other kids because they were born into a wealthier family?
   Yes   No

7. Do your kids complain when you ask them to do something for you?
   Yes   No

8. Do you give them the things they want without expecting that they earn them (through chores, schoolwork, good behavior, etc.)?
   Yes   No

9. Do your children seem dissatisfied, gloomy, bored, apprehensive, restless?
   Yes   No

10. Do you give them things to make them happy—only to be
    dismayed that they are more miserable than ever?
    Yes   No

For each Yes, score 1 point. For each No, score 0.

- If you scored 3 or less, you've done a great job of protecting
  your kids from developing a sense of entitlement.
- A score from 4-8 suggests caution: this score indicates that your
  children are suffering from a "me, me" attitude. Read further
  and stay alert to this issue, lest it become a bigger problem.
- A score above 8 strongly indicates that your kids have an entitlement orientation—and the problems that go with it. It's
  not too late to correct this if you're willing to confront it
  now.

Getting Out of the Way: Wealth as a Real-World Insulator

Kids of any income level can develop a sense of narcissistic entitlement if their parents are indulgent enough, and if nothing is expected
of them in return. But this particular symptom is directly tied to
wealth: the higher the family's bottom line, the more incidences of narcissistic entitlement you're likely to find—and the more acute these
cases will be. In the children of the super-wealthy, the risks are magni-
fied, particularly if the parents were also raised with a sense that their
money made them "special."

Compounding the entitlement that grows from over-indulgence
is the insulation that often stands between wealthy children and the
rest of the world. Private schools, chauffeurs, elite clubs, and so forth
ensure that rich kids will have few opportunities for direct contact
with the outside world. They may have no chance to discover that
non-wealthy kids are just kids—no better, no worse. They may never
discover the connection between effort and reward, between work and
money. And they may never develop a sense of the complexities of cir-

cumstance, luck, experience, education, and an endless array of other factors that land people where they are in the socioeconomic equation.

These pampered children may never meet the dedicated special ed teacher who makes a modest but adequate $24,000 a year, and lives a more richly rewarding life than most wealthy kids will ever know. They may not encounter the child whose mother works three jobs in a valiant effort to pay for her husband's $600,000 open-heart surgery, which health insurance refused to cover. In their plush private colleges, they're unlikely to bump into the fiery grad student who's living on rice and hot dogs and dreams of a better tomorrow. Rich kids may know nothing more than the company of other rich kids—a poor venue to discover one's true place in the world.

Rx # 3: Breaking the Back of Entitlement

Step #1: Check Yourself

Before you even broach the subject with your kids, make sure you're setting the right example. Kids have an extremely sensitive B.S. meter and any hypocrisy on your part will set it off.

Parents need to help their children to see that even though they may be unique in some ways, they are no more "special" than any other human being. But they'll never accept this lesson from you if they see you acting as though you're better than everyone else. Do you demand special treatment at restaurants, break in line at the movies, or expect deferential service at the Mercedes dealership? Do you like being treated like the Big Cheese? Do you throw your name around? Do you flaunt your wealth? If so, you're part of the problem.

Your kids are watching. If you catch yourself doing these types of behaviors, cut it out.

Step #2: Put Them On Notice

Sit your kids down and tell them that you don't like the attitude you're seeing, and inform them that you're going to make some changes.

Your talk might go something like this, "Your dad and I have realized that we've given you the wrong impression about your place in the world. We've allowed you to get the idea that our money makes us better than other people, and that's simply not the case. We've made a lot of mistakes that have allowed you to develop this attitude, and now we're going to have to make some changes to try to fix it."

Describe exactly what will change and why. Tell them what you expect from them. Describe to your kids the specific behaviors that you want to see changed. For example, they're to be considerate and politely greet and thank the people serving them in shops and restaurants, not jump lines at the movies and concerts, and address others by their preferred name no matter what the situation. The Golden Rule applies to the wealthy as well. Above all they need to learn to treat others as they themselves wish to be treated.

Step #3: Post No Bail.

Wealthy parents have the resources to buy their kids' way out of any unpleasant situation—that doesn't mean that it's ethical to do so. Money doesn't absolve us of the consequences of our actions. *Don't send the message that money gives them this kind of immunity!*

When your children get themselves into trouble, let them be accountable to real world consequences. This means no "get home free" passes. By refusing to cushion them from the results of their own behavior, you're helping them learn that the same rules of life that apply to everyone else also apply to them.

Strip them of the status they're accustomed to enjoying because of their money—or at least, minimize it as much as you can. Ask principals, teachers, police officers, employees and relatives to help you with this: your children should not be shown deference because of their socioeconomic level. Don't let anything get between your child and real-world experiences, their best teachers.

Step #4: Make Them Learn to Earn.

Many parents drop the ball on this issue; they end up with kids who expect everything and give nothing. End the "free lunch" program that encourages entitlement. The world doesn't owe them a living. Make your kids earn what they get.

Start this with kids of any age, but brace yourself for a bigger backlash if your kid's already in their teens! The longer parents wait to start, the tougher it is to correct—but it's still their responsibility to do so.

Give them a chance to learn to earn. Have them do things that strengthen the connection between effort and reward. Use allowances to link money to effort and work. Give them a taste of real labor, and its benefits. Encourage your pre-teens to run lemonade stands, wash cars and do the neighbors' yard work to earn cash. Urge your teenagers to get part-time jobs, particularly during summer break. Insist that adult children work full-time, or pursue college full-time, if they're going to stay at home.

Should you give your kids jobs in the family business? Let me offer a word of caution about that. Such positions are often breeding grounds for more entitlement. It's not a real job if Junior writes his own job description, comes to work whenever he feels like it, demands an exorbitant salary, and stirs up resentment among the other employees. It's tough for a kid to rid himself of the taint of "specialness" when everybody walks on eggshells around him because he's the boss's kid.

If you consider this a learning-earning experience, think again. Do your kids a favor they'll thank you for years from now. Fire them today, boot them out of the company, let them find a new job completely on their own, and let them work in the real world for at least two years. If they make a go of it, and their attitude improves, you can think about hiring them back, but only if they've got something positive to bring to your company.

Step #5: Show Them Other Shoes.

Do things that help your kids build empathy for the feelings of others and an appreciation of other people's experiences. Entitled kids lack any real concern for what others feel; they only care about their own feelings. Don't doom them to living in a universe of one.

It's easier to teach empathy to preteens. Talk openly to your young child about your own feelings while encouraging expression of their own emotions. Comment on the similarities and differences between the two sets of feelings. Point out the fact that other people may feel differently than they do, and that's okay.

You might say to your sobbing four-year old on the playground, "Billy, I feel sad seeing John hit you in the stomach, but look over there. I think Johnny's feeling the same way from where you pushed him off the slide." If we talk to them, kids can learn empathy for others at a fairly young age. Once they learn it, constantly reinforce it.

As always, the adolescent is a different animal. I can't count how many parents, in seminars or in my office, have said, "Susie only cares for Susie. If we didn't provide her meal ticket, she wouldn't know we existed." Adolescents don't seem to care about anybody outside of themselves and their tight circle of friends. It's not pretty, but it's normal. You were a teenager once; you remember how it was. Take heart: most kids and parents survive. Fortunately, most teenagers eventually outgrow their extreme narcissism and become decent human beings.

Even during this self-centered phase, you can do a few things to encourage your teenager's emotional sensitivity. Keep in mind, though, that for the most part, you'll be planting seeds that will lie dormant until the storm of adolescence subsides. Don't expect dazzling results overnight. Keep on discussing your feelings with them, and keep the dialogue going about the diversity of other people's feelings. Give them firm guidelines for the kind of respect you expect them to show to others—especially to other family members. When they behave rudely, calmly let them know. If they're testing you—-and they will—don't react. You're the parent. Hold firm, or you'll lose both the lesson and their respect.

Expose them to people of other ethnic backgrounds, circumstances and socioeconomic levels. If your kids go to an exclusive private school, they may rarely bump into children outside their elite circle. Get them involved in sports, classes or clubs through your local community center, where they'll meet a broader variety of people. Take them to visit different neighborhoods; occasionally, attend religious services in a non-affluent community. Go on family field trips to events in other communities: Juneteenth celebrations, Cinco de Mayo festivals, Native American pow-wows. Take them to visit the elderly in nursing homes, to cuddle AIDS babies in hospital wards.

Introduce them to real-life heroes: share with them the stories of people who rose from dire hardship to accomplish great feats. Show them what it *really* means to be special!

When they've been exposed to the larger panoply of human experience, your kids will have a more realistic grasp of their place in it.

Step #6: Have Them Give Till it Hurts:

Giving is one of the best antidotes for entitlement. Since entitlement is a one-way street, you may have to pave a new lane for reciprocity by urging your kids to give back. Start as early as possible. If you have young children, teach them that they must contribute to the household by doing small chores, doing special things for others, saying thank you, and donating a portion of their allowance to church or charity, which we'll cover in more detail in a later chapter.

As your kids get older, provide them with opportunities to do these things on a larger scale. In a number of families, parents require their middle-school-aged kids to become altar servers at church: "It's our duty to God." You might also present young adolescents with opportunities to run neighborhood charity drives, or to collect canned food for their local food bank. High school students and young adults have even greater opportunities for giving. Your kids will reap phenomenal growth from youth volunteer programs that will bring them face to face with needy people from all walks of life. One summer filled with these kinds of eye-openers may turn your Silver Spooner around.

I can't emphasize this point enough. Giving advantaged kids chances to help others should be as fundamental to their upbringing as enrolling them in school. It's perfectly fine to insist that a small portion of a child's money be donated to a church, charity or cause, whichever they decide. Tell them, "We're fortunate to have more than we need, so we have to understand that what we have extra is not just for us. We can use it to help others. That's our responsibility."

For the hard-case adolescent whose narcissistic attitude is in full bloom, start by making any extra privileges strictly contingent upon giving: if they don't put in time on community service projects, or in the family's philanthropic endeavors, they don't get to go on that all-important spring break ski trip.

You might argue that involuntary philanthropy doesn't count because it doesn't come from a "true spirit of giving." Okay, but how many years do you plan to hang around waiting for the "giving spirit" to hit? Sometimes people need to do the behavior in order to get to the feeling they're looking for. Start with the 'outside-in' approach: push them to give, and hope that it takes. It's better than bratty entitlement.

Step #7: Support Selflessness.

Catch them being good and jump on it. Find opportunities to support and encourage your child's involvement in activities that require real effort and a positive external focus. Identify their specific interests and passions (saving the whales, sheltering the homeless—whatever they have an inclination toward) and then help them link these to the kinds of organizations and activities that can involve them.

It's important that you attend meetings and functions with them to get them started. If you get the chance, work alongside them in the activity. Praise them for their good works. Constantly keep an eye out for these opportunities and actively show your appreciation any time an act of selflessness pops up on your philanthropic radar screen. They may not show it—and if they're adolescents, they may intentionally *avoid* showing it—but your involvement and positive attention will mean the world to them.

Let me offer one last note on the narcissistically entitled. The older your kids get, the more set they become in their ways. The younger you can catch them, the better. If your kids are grown up, you'll have a harder task in front of you. And unfortunately, not every Silver Spooner can be rescued. Adults who are severely "empathetically challenged" aren't likely to respond to these prescriptions, nor for that matter, to outside counseling. Therapy requires motivation for change, which the adult Silver Spooner isn't likely to have. Don't close the door on hope, at any age, but understand that the older your adult Spooner gets, the more likely you're looking not at a cure, but at damage control. I'll speak more to this in a later chapter.

Chapter Seven:

Do Teach Them Money Management: The Law of Fiscal Responsibility

Money is a terrible master, but an excellent servant.
—P. T. Barnum

The Importance of Age-Appropriate Financial Skills

The American dream is dead—at least, the one that drove our parents in the post-war generation. Our children can't expect to land a secure job straight out of high school, settle into it for forty-five years, and retire comfortably with a gold watch and a small fortune in the bank. Our means of generating income have become far more precarious, while our appetite for material goods has burgeoned. Today's generation doesn't have time to grow rich slowly—they want it now!

The pursuit of money and material goods has replaced the simple joys of family life that typified the 1950s and before. According to the Maryland-based Center for a New American Dream, which dispenses advice for families trapped in raging consumerism, two-thirds of parents say their kids define their self-worth in terms of possessions; half say their children prefer to go to a shopping mall than to go hiking on a family outing; and a majority admit to buying their kids products they disapprove of because the kids said they "needed" the items to fit in with their friends. Money plays a larger role than ever in young people's lives, yet its *presence* in their lives has become far more mercurial.

Affluent parents today are justifiably concerned that their children will not fare as well as they have financially. In fact, the odds are definitely stacked against them. This is why it's imperative that parents teach their children how to manage money responsibly, and show them the reason for doing so. It's our job to impart both the knowledge and the desire.

If we don't arm our kids with financial street smarts, no amount of money will be safe with them. Any size fortune can be squandered.

Conversely, if they respect money, and manage it judiciously, they can achieve financial stability on an amount far less than a fortune.

How well do your children handle money? Do they treat it like Kleenex? Do they have difficulty saving, budgeting, paying bills? The following test is designed to gauge your child's financial aptitude. Since our children's relationship to money changes profoundly over the course of their growing-up years, I've designed one test for kids ages 6 to 12, and a separate test for adolescents and young adults, ages 13 and up:

Self-Test: Are You Teaching Your Young Child Money Management? (Ages 6 to 12)

1. Do your young children think money grows on trees—are they unaware of the link between work and income?
   Yes   No

2. Do your children expect regular handouts of cash on demand—in addition to their allowance?
   Yes   No

3. Does your child have a perpetually empty piggy bank or savings account?
   Yes   No

4. Is your child hooked on trendy, faddish items?
   Yes   No

5. Do your children habitually blow all their cash on impulse purchases?
   Yes   No

6. Is your child struggling to understand the concept of saving up for a large purchase?

   Yes   No

7. Do you shy away from talking about money with your children?

   Yes   No

8. Do you exclude your children from family financial chores (bill-paying, budgeting, account management, consumer decision-making, etc.)?

   Yes   No

9. Do you keep putting off teaching them how to balance a checkbook, handle a credit card, build a savings account, or manage investments?

   Yes   No

10. Do you believe financial issues are inappropriate subject matter for young children?

    Yes   No

For each Yes, score 1 point. For each No, score 0.

- Congratulations! A score of 2 or lower suggests your child has developed a basic understanding of money management.
- A score from 4-8 is reason for concern if your child is approaching adolescence. If this gap in their knowledge is not addressed soon, it will set the stage for graver problems.
- A score above 8 indicates that your children are developing serious deficits in their financial skills. Now is the time to act, before outside influences begin to eclipse your parental authority!

Self-Test: Are You Teaching Your Adolescent/Young Adult Money Management? (Ages 13 and up.)

1. Does money seem to slip right through your child's fingers?

   Yes   No

2. Does your child treat a credit card like a bottomless well of money?
   Yes   No

3. Does your child have a history of overdrawn accounts and unpaid bills?
   Yes   No

4. Does your child make poor consumer choices (buying on impulse, buying trendy items that will be obsolete next week, paying too much)?
   Yes   No

5. Are you afraid that your children will ruin their credit ratings?
   Yes   No

6. Are you worried that your children don't understand the concept of living within their means?
   Yes No

7. Do you shy away from talking about money with your children?
   Yes No

8. Do you exclude your children from financial chores (bill-paying, budgeting, account management, consumer decision-making, etc.)?
   Yes No

9. Do you keep putting off teaching them how to balance a checkbook, handle a credit card, build a savings account, or manage investments?
   Yes No

10. Do you shelter your children from the results of their poor money management?
    Yes No

For each Yes, score 1 point. For each No, score 0.

- Congratulations! A score of 2 or lower suggests that your child has developed a basic understanding of money issues and management.

- A score from 4-8 is reason for some concern, particularly for the adult child. Chances are your kids need some remedial education and experience in this area.
- Time for major catch up. A score above 8 points to deficiencies in both fiscal knowledge and skills, something that can significantly affect your child's ability to function adequately in the larger world. Don't panic—in a moment I'll provide a crash course to raise their fiscal IQ.

If your kids tested poorly in this area, join the club. Many of today's children are woefully ignorant about money. They only know of one thing to do with it!

Financial ignorance becomes a bigger problem over time. The bad money-management habits our kids learned in childhood may cost them the solid credit rating they need to become homeowners when they reach adulthood, and may even leave them destitute when they reach retirement age!

Wealthy families face an especially delicate task in teaching children about money. John D. Rockefeller, convinced that struggle was the crucible of character, was determined to instill in his children the same values and lessons of his threadbare boyhood. Besides concealing the magnitude of his fortune, Rockefeller created a make-believe market economy where the children earned pocket money by performing chores. They earned two cents for killing flies, ten cents for sharpening pencils, five cents per hour for practicing their musical instruments, and a dollar for repairing vases. Both acutely aware of other rich children spoiled by their parents, John Sr, and his wife Cettie never missed an opportunity to teach their children the relationship between effort and reward.

Even if their fortunes don't match the Rockefellers,' parents must be responsible for teaching their kids how to properly manage their finances. But that's only half of the job. We must also show them the reason for doing so. I've encountered plenty of financially astute adult children, some of them bankers and business managers, who were miserable money-handlers. They knew how to manage money, but they saw no reason to do so.

The following prescription will help you address both sides of the money management coin: it will not only help you arm your children with the financial skills they need; it will also bring them face to face with the consequences they'll suffer if they don't put those skills to use. As with the diagnostic test, I've divided these exercises by age. The first, for children twelve and under, is primarily a guide to preventing financial illiteracy. The second is a remedy for teens and young adults who've already made a few financial blunders.

Rx # 4 Junior: Developing Your Child's Financial IQ

Step #1: Show Them You Know

As always, the first task is to start modeling the behavior you're looking for in your children. Set the right example. Show your kids how to handle money well by your own spending, saving and giving behaviors. Be sure the kinds of things you're doing with money are things you want your kids to emulate. If not, get your own financial house in order first.

Begin with the basics at the earliest age possible by talking in simple terms about what you're doing when you write a check, visit the bank or ATM, make a purchase at the store, tithe, make a charitable contribution, or use your credit card. Keep the complexity of your explanations age appropriate. Don't try to explain the ins and outs of adjustable rate mortgages to your five-year old any more than you'd talk to your teenager about how many dimes make up a dollar.

Be aware that little eyes are watching and little ears are listening to every thing you say and do. Never underestimate the power of your good example. Remember, monkey sees, monkey does.

Step #2: Financial Fun

Whenever possible, make your money lessons fun and interesting. This is particularly important for younger children, many of whom have the attention span of a gnat. They won't learn anything from dry, boring lectures. Instead, put your financial lessons into action!

One wealthy client I spoke with had a rather creative way of educating his two children, ages ten and twelve, about money. He started a family investment club. He gathered the kids together and informed them they each had $1000 to invest and it was their sole responsibility to research and pick a company. The youngest, who was quite the tinkerer, picked Lowes Home Improvement, while his elder sister, a blossoming fashion bug, chose the Gap. Over the next months, as they watched their small fortunes rise and fall, the kids learned about the dangers and risks of stocks and the vagaries of the markets— as well as ways to deal with their feelings about money.

Sometimes you can get their competitive juices flowing by offering challenges: how cheaply can they buy a particular item they want? How much interest will they accrue if they sock their money away in a CD, versus an old-fashioned savings account? Wherever you can, tie these lessons to the things that interest them: jewelry, gadgets, CDs—whatever floats their boats.

Step #3: Muting Madison's Madness

Our kids are constantly bombarded by Madison Avenue's deafening drumbeat – buy, buy, buy. Although it's nearly impossible to turn down the volume, parents can channel these messages into financial lessons for their kids.

Challenge your kids: "You want a PlayStation? Where did that desire come from? You mean you didn't have a desire for that thing before you saw that ad? What did that ad tell you? What benefits do you think you'd get from owning it?" Help them recognize when their decisions are based on realistic expectations or pure fantasy. This is your chance to teach them to be more conscious consumers.

Many of the wealthy people I've met, besides being hard workers and good savers, are extremely savvy consumers. They don't fall into mindless consumption; instead, they research big purchases and think twice about small ones. Not a bad financial lesson to teach your children.

Step #4: Set the Bar

Children are helped – not hurt – by the establishment of parental standards and boundaries. In fact, they desperately need them, at least as much as food, water, and shelter. So don't disappoint. Communicate directly the expectations you have for your children.

As you talk about money and finances openly, at the same time tell your children exactly what they can expect from you and what is their responsibility to handle on their own. Setting expectations and holding them accountable pushes kids to develop the kind of fiscal knowledge and skills they may not otherwise. But don't assume they know what your expectations are. Be absolutely explicit.

For example, if you expect your seven-year old to use his allowance money to buy things he wants, let him know. If your teenager has to start paying her own car insurance after graduating from high school, spell it out. You want to make sure your expectations are reasonable, but once you decide this, don't waffle. It's confusing to children and sends the wrong message.

Step #5: Practice Makes Perfect

Don't get me wrong; nobody's *perfect*. But good practice and learning come more from experience than lectures. The older the child, the truer this becomes. So offer your children plenty of real-world practice opportunities to solidify what they've learned. Be sure to give your kids actual opportunities to handle money—preferably their own—every chance you get. Then do the hardest thing that good parents do: stand back and let them learn from their own mistakes. That's good practice, the kind of practice that teaches lessons kids never forget.

Rx # 4 for Teens and Adults: Correcting Financial Illiteracy

Step #1: Own Up

If you've waited until your kids are well into adolescence—or, God forbid, beyond—to begin their financial education, we're probably looking at damage control rather than prevention. It's a more painful way to learn these lessons, but it's better than nothing!

One of my clients told me that when she was growing up her father often berated her for not knowing the value of a dollar. "But Dr. Buffone," she added, "He never *taught* me anything about the value of a dollar! The only time he ever mentioned money was to criticize me for not knowing anything about it!"

If your kids are approaching adulthood and you've never shown them so much as a balanced checkbook, don't blame them for their reckless financial habits! Admit your mistake: "I'm afraid we've waited too long to help you learn the things you should know about money. We've put you in the position of having to play catch-up, and we're sorry about that. But we've got to make sure you understand these skills, now that you're going into the world. We want you to know how to handle money, because good financial habits will save you from a world of hurt once you're on your own."

Step #2: Repair the Damage

Day One of their new, responsible financial lives should be spent developing a plan to fix whatever damage they've done. Are we looking at a cell phone bill that's three months overdue or stacked with hefty long-distance charges? Sorting through a stack of maxed-out credit cards? A mountain of checks stamped "non-sufficient funds"?

Start off on the right foot. Have them make a list of all their debts, the age of the debt, the amount, and the current state of the account. Encourage them to call up their creditors, to settle with them on repayment arrangements. Help them develop a strategy for paying off those overdue bills, even if it will take them quite a while—even if they must take on an extra job to whittle those debts back down.

Guide them, help them get the basic principles down, help them construct a plan, but whatever you do, *don't bail them out!* Do that, and they will learn nothing from the whole experience, except that they can do whatever they want and you'll always be there, checkbook in hand, ready to fix it for them!

Step #3: Enroll Them in Money 101

Now that their financial lives are on the mend, give them the tools they need to avoid such entanglements in the future. Make sure they have a firm grasp of basic money management principles.

Explain to them the concept of living and spending beneath their means. Help them set up a budget for their expenses and track their expenditures with them for the first few months.

Show them concretely the reasons why people must pay their bills on time. Explain their credit rating to them; tell them about the difficulty they'll have in securing a house, a car, or a job if they ruin their financial reputation.

Warn them about the misuse of credit cards. Break out the calculator and show them the vast amounts of money they could waste in interest charges. Teach them sensible borrowing: make sure they know how interest works. Help them to understand that borrowing money only makes sense when it's for things that appreciate in value, like a house or an education.

Give them the basics of saving and investing. Show them the magic of compounding. Stress the importance of putting money away for a rainy day.

Step #4: Give Them a Reason to Learn It

If your adolescent and young adult kids have gotten this far along without basic financial skills, they may not yet recognize the need for them. These lessons are unlikely to take unless your children see money as a limited resource. Are they accustomed to letting money flow through their hands like water? If so, it's time to close the tap.

Chapter Eight:

Do Practice What You Preach: The Law of Example

Money buys everything except love, personality,
freedom, immortality, silence, peace.
—Carl Sandburg

Values Are Contagious: What Are You Passing On?

What kind of messages do you send your children about money? What does your behavior tell them about the relationship of money to happiness? If you were to ask your kids what they believe you stand for, what you value most in your life, what would they say?

Do *you* know what matters most in your life? If you're unsure of your own values and priorities, now's the time to check your focus. Because whether you know your true values or not, the messages your behavior sends to your kids are coming through loud and clear. If you're always sounding off about the importance of family, yet you work ninety-hour weeks, what are you really communicating to your kids? If you preach against the mindless pursuit of the almighty dollar but are constantly drooling over the neighbors' new Mercedes, what are you really saying?

Parents, without even knowing it, often slip up and send mixed signals. No wonder our kids are confused.

I see this all the time. Parents take their teenagers to Aspen for two weeks of skiing, then berate them for piddling away their $20 allowance on movies. They buy their kids $150 sneakers to wear to school, but chide them for wanting an expensive set of CDs. They give their child a $30,000 SUV, then complain about having to pay for the gasoline. Kids see exactly who you are and what you feel is important, no matter how hard you may try to fool yourself—or them.

The following test provides you with an opportunity to check out your own financial integrity:

Self-Test: Do You Practice What You Preach?

1. Do your kids believe that the latest toy, gadget or fashion will make them happy?
   Yes   No
2. Do they buy things in order to feel better about themselves?
   Yes   No
3. Do they shop to relieve boredom, loneliness, stress or depression?
   Yes   No
4. Do your children obsessively compare what they have to what other kids have?
   Yes   No
5. Do your children look down on other kids for what they don't have?
   Yes   No
6. Do your children have little regard for the work it takes to make and keep money?
   Yes   No
7. Do your children observe you trying to "keep up with the Joneses"?
   Yes   No
8. Do you choose certain designer labels, types of cars or snooty restaurants because of what they "say" about you?
   Yes   No

9. Do you eschew wholesale outlets and discount stores to avoid being seen "buying the cheap stuff"?
   Yes   No
10. Do you measure a person's worth by their wealth?
   Yes   No

For each Yes, score 1 point. For each No, score 0.

- A score of 2 or less suggests that your kids have found a good balance: they neither undervalue nor overvalue material wealth.
- Be alert if your score falls between 4-8. Your children may be overly preoccupied with money and possessions. Time to follow the prescriptions outlined in this chapter to set your correction course.
- Be concerned if your score tops 8. Chances are your kids have gone overboard materially and have lost any sense of your most cherished values. Act immediately to establish damage control.

I Can't Hear You: Actions Speak Louder Than Words

Our financial values can have a direct impact on our overall happiness. It can be tremendously liberating to live beneath our means—and emotionally devastating to live above them!

When we spend less than we make, and sock away or invest the excess, our financial health is always growing rosier. We never lie awake at night worrying whether we'll be able to make that credit card payment before they report us to a collection agency! Living beneath our means—one of the pinnacles of sound financial values—puts us in a position of power.

By contrast, living above our means puts us in a position of weakness. When our spending outstrips our income, we feel underpaid, put-upon, beaten up by taxes and inflation. We end up grousing about the price of milk and gas. We feel forever uneasy, because we never know if there will be enough cash to cover this month's expenses. We watch our debts mounting, and bemoan the high interest rates our creditors charge us. We blame our stingy bosses, the greedy IRS, the lousy economy—everyone but ourselves!

If we want to bring our behavior in line with our financial values we must start by examining our perspective, our internal frame of reference. Happiness is a head job. No matter what our income level, we can gain a healthier perspective by cutting out the poor talk:

Instead of saying "I need that" we can say, "I want that."

"I don't make enough money" can become "I spend more than I make."

"We can't afford it" becomes "We choose to spend our money on other things."

"Why can't my parents help me" turns into "What can I do to help myself?"

Usually we don't really need what we covet, but lapse into spending more than we have. We can afford many things, if they're really important to us. We've simply had other things we've spent our money on. We decide every day what's important. The choice is ours. "We can't afford it" denies this choice and turns us into self-pitying victims.

Are you conscious of the way you relate to money in your own life? No matter your net worth, do you fall into poor talk, feeling that your finances are out of your control? What lessons are you teaching your children by your example? Have you taken too much responsibility for your children's welfare by buying them out of difficult jams? Are your true values and priorities reflected in your spending patterns?

Check the messages you're sending your own kids. Be sure they're positive and in line with what you wish them to learn. Be clear and consistent in what you teach. Because we can't really expect children to do "as we say and not as we do."

Rx #5: Modeling A Healthy Relationship to Money

Step #1: Values Check

Begin by assessing your own values. Whether you realize it or not, your values are like a compass, helping to guide your everyday decisions and ultimately shaping your entire life. But your personal values don't just steer *your* direction on life's highway. Whether you realize it or not, there are little passengers in the car with you. Your personal values, good and bad, are likely to be transmitted directly to your children, and to their children, and so on. Don't take your values lightly. It's your responsibility as a parent to consciously communicate what you value, and to make sure that these values are consistent with word and deed.

Take a moment right now and think about your values. What is most important to you? Is it health, integrity, power, status, family, peace, success, or honor? List below your five most cherished values:

1.
2.
3.
4.
5.

Now ask yourself honestly: are you living your life according to these values? Are your spending habits and lifestyle consistent with them? Be sure your inner values are consistently reflected in your outer behavior. If they're not, the first thing you need to do is set a correction course to line up your behavior with what you say is important.

Step #2: Roll In The Roles

Parents are their children's most significant role models, of course. But you can reinforce the values you wish to instill by exposing them to healthy, respectable exemplars who will help them learn appropriate financial values. These could be slightly older peers, relatives or family friends. Grandparents, who often have extra time and love for their grandchildren, often are excellent candidates for mentoring as long as they're willing to play by your rules. This step can be effective for kids throughout adulthood.

Step #3: Provide Perspective

Help your children see your financial values in a variety of contexts. Spell out both the promises and the problems of prosperity in ways that your kids can understand. Explain the advantages and the challenges of having more wealth than other people. Help them deal with the emotional side of the issue by openly discussing their feelings, and your own, about having what you have and how this is received in the larger world. They may feel guilty because of their wealth; others may feel jealous and resentful. Teach your children to talk frankly about these feelings, and encourage them to search for ways to resolve them.

Step #4: Take the emphasis off externals

Don't dwell on them verbally or through your actions, as we often see in the conspicuous consumption of the well off. Just because you can buy anything doesn't mean it's good to do so. Watch and minimize your own unnecessary, and often mindless, consumption. Is it really necessary to buy a new model Mercedes every year, or worse yet, tell everyone about it? Do you really have to have a new Rolex when the old one still keeps good time? Closely monitor other powerful influences such as the media, and work to counter messages pushing excess and extravagance.

Step #5: The Best Laid Plans…

If your children have hit their late twenties or older, take a good look, because what you see is pretty much what you've got. If your chronologically adult kids are still partying constantly, jumping jobs, gobbling up money, and lacking a moral compass, there's very little you can do at this point to change them. It's time to back off and stop trying to force them to follow in your footsteps.

Values tend to gel early, solidify in late adolescence, and become concrete by the late twenties. If you missed the window of opportunity, don't despair. You may still offer a positive influence. Stay your course; continue to live the values that you feel are important. Be sure these values are reflected in any gifts, wills, trusts, and family foundations. Don't count on a miracle, but don't lose hope. Follow the laws we've discussed. There's always a chance that they'll come around of their own volition, once they've had several years of reality under their belts.

PART THREE:

LIVING THE LAWS
FROM CRADLE TO GRAVE

By now you're familiar with the Five Laws of Financial Parenting. You've identified your child's problem areas and implemented the corrective prescriptions outlined in the previous chapters. Now, we're going to expand the realm of the Five Laws across time.

If your children are quite young, we'll look at a strategy that will keep the dreaded Silver Spoon Syndrome from getting a claw-hold on them. If they're approaching adolescence, we'll discuss some of the special financial concerns this inherently rebellious, me-focused phase brings to the fore. If your children are in their late teens, twenties, or early thirties, we'll examine the Five Laws in the light of their blossoming adulthood. If your adult children are approaching mid-life and are becoming set in their ways, we'll discuss the sensitive issues of family business succession and inheritance.

To conclude, we'll take in the big picture. We'll examine the true legacy you wish to leave behind for your children—both the material and the non-material bequests—which will make up the final measurement of your success.

Chapter Nine:

From 3 to 12:
Preventing the Silver Spoon Syndrome

She was born with an entire silver
dinner service in her mouth.
—Clive James of Grace Kelly

"My children are still young, so I want to instill the right values now, before it's too late," said Beth Moss, mother of two preschoolers. "I've seen a lot of our friends turn their kids into spoiled rotten brats whom I can't stand to be around. These are the critical years and I don't want to make the kind of mistakes that we'll have to live with for the rest of our lives."

The Mosses aren't alone in their concern. A 2001 Time/CNN poll found that 80% of people think kids today are more spoiled than kids 10 or 15 years ago. Two-thirds of parents admit that their *own* kids are spoiled. From $25,000 catered birthday bashes for six-year olds to actress Carrie Fisher buying her nine-year old daughter an elephant for her birthday, parents are setting new records when it comes to indulging their children.

Spoiling is easier to do than to undo. But fortunately if your children are six years old or younger, you're in luck. At this age, we're still talking more about prevention than about damage control.

When do parents need to start brat-proofing their kids? Most experts agree that babies under six months can't be spoiled. Picking them up when they cry, and indeed, catering to their every need can't spoil them. It's only after the child reaches six months that parents need to worry.

Beth and Jake Moss, both high-end earners, decided to start a brat-proofing regimen when their children were still preschoolers. Most experts would support this idea of instilling the habits of hard work and thrift at an earlier age. Emily, age three, and David, age five, like all kids their age, were like little sponges, ready to soak up whatever lessons Mom and Dad offered. It was simply up to the parents to figure out the lesson plan.

The Mosses faced two daunting challenges. First, in order to teach their children effectively, they had to become proficient in the subject of finance—an area that the majority of Americans admit they don't understand well. Second, they had to overcome their reluctance to discuss money.

"My parents never brought up money, like it was some dirty word. I never knew what they earned, what they paid for things, why I got an allowance when I did, or what was expected of me as I grew up," said Beth. "It was a mystery. The unwritten rule was that we just didn't talk about it. I've been in the dark about financial matters most of my life. Jake's family was the same way, so we've played a lot of catch-up as adults. I don't want my kids to repeat the same cycle. I want to teach them it's alright to talk about money and learn how to manage it."

Financial parenting doesn't have to be boring, for you or your children. In fact, for these lessons to really take hold, the process of learning and applying these principles must be fun. First we'll talk about teaching children specific money skills and then we'll focus on educating them in the larger life lessons, the lessons of character.

Inoculating Your Young Child Against "Affluenza"

Before we start planning the financial talks we want to have with our kids, we must recall Law #5, and make certain that we are willing to practice what we preach.

"Jake and I realize that we're going to have to change a few things if we're going to set a good example," Beth admitted, "We're still over-spending, and that causes some stress and conflicts. We've agreed to get our own financial house in order to make sure we're living what we teach."

Many of us could stand to follow Beth and Jake's lead. Most Americans are miserable savers, and not much better as consumers. The average American saves between 4 to 6 percent of their annual income. That leaves, on average after taxes, about 65 percent of their income to cover the costs of living. The task of saving is no more difficult than that of spending. It's just that spending is a heck of a lot more fun.

Before you have that first financial conversation with your child, make sure you're setting the right example. If you want your kids to learn to manage money responsibly, set aside savings for the future, give to charity, and be able to live within their means, be certain you're first doing all these things yourself.

Otherwise, don't be surprised when your kids figure out that you're full of hot air. And they will. Take a look in the mirror. Are your values and financial practices clear and consistent? Are they what you want your kids to follow? If so, congratulate yourself. You're already halfway through Show and Tell.

It's never too soon to start working on the 4th Law of Financial Parenting: giving kids sound financial knowledge and the desire to use it.

For the youngest children, the very first step involves explaining what money is. By playing a few simple money recognition games, you can teach your preschooler the different kinds of coins and bills, and the principle of exchanging money for the things they want. Set up a pretend candy shop or pet store. Take turns being the customer or the shop owner. Use real cash, not play money, to give your child a feel for the genuine article. Neale Godfrey in *Money Doesn't Grow On Trees* and *A Penny Saved* offers a number of these practical, fun exercises to help parents teach the money basics.

Once children can recognize the different kinds of money, and understand that it is exchanged for things they want, they're ready to start on the fiscal fundamentals: saving and spending.

Parents only need a couple of tools to teach these fundamentals; a savings plan and a spending plan. The saving part always comes first. For young children, we usually teach these lessons by introducing them to their first economy, an allowance.

The First Economy: The Do's and Don't's of Allowances

What exactly is involved in setting up a savings plan for a child? First we have to give our children the opportunity to get their hands on some money. I recommend that kids be given an allowance—preferably one that is earned. Next, they need a place to keep their money, like a jar, purse, wallet or piggy bank. Finally, they need you to teach them what to *do* with the money, and consistently offer the encouragement and support to stick with the plan.

Learning to save money is like learning any new behavior. Take shoe tying: when children are ready, you first tell them why shoe laces need tying, then show how to tie the laces, and finally, help them do it themselves. Once they succeed in tying the laces on their own, you step back and praise them for successfully completing the task.

You'll go through the same process teaching your children to save money. First, explain in simple terms what saving is. Demonstrating with real life illustrations they can understand. For example, Beth might tell her kids that saving is taking something and putting it aside for later. She might use examples like fruit juice or animal crackers, which the children may set aside on the counter to enjoy after their walk.

Next, Beth might talk about what's good about saving. She could show how she saves gift boxes after Christmas wrapping to use again, how they save newspapers for recycling, colored paperclips or buttons, or their baby clothes to give to a friend. Point out some examples of saving that your kids can relate to their everyday experience. Like any good teacher, you must bring the concept alive through examples.

Though adults may save for large goals like retirement and college, don't expect your five-year-old to get wild about putting money away for his freshman year at the state university. Young kids need to see fun, immediate benefits to saving. Help them save up for a moderately priced toy that they really want, something that they can achieve quickly enough that this first lesson doesn't become tedious.

A simple saving program offers a triple benefit. First, kids learn the importance of earning money to get what they want. Second, they learn the discipline of deferring gratification by putting money aside for specific goals. Third, they enjoy the pleasure of accomplishing something through their own efforts. These experiences are doing far more than flexing a child's financial muscles. They're also forming the building blocks of character.

Remember that the act of saving money is *learned*; none of us are born with it. We, too, had to be taught to tie our shoes. It took practice, and it helped if we got consistent praise along the way. Once we attained a bit of success, and the satisfaction of accomplishment kicked in, it became easier. So, too, with our kids' savings habits: after a while, they'll be old hands at putting money aside, and the intrinsic pride and rewards their savings bring them will take over the job for us.

But how will they earn those first hefty quarters that make such a delicious *plunk* going into the piggy bank? Let's give them a job.

First establish the allowance amount, or "salary." This needs to be age-appropriate and enough to mean something to the child. One suggested rule of thumb is one dollar for every year of their age, so a 3 year old gets $3, a 5 year old $5, and so on. Some parents pay a little less and some more. Just don't go overboard on the amount. I've met some kids who get higher weekly allowances than many adults earn at skilled jobs! Don't make it ridiculously high or you create a false economy and unrealistic expectations. Whatever amount you decide on, be consistent. Don't let your kids argue or negotiate the amount once it's been set.

Some parents chafe at paying their kids an allowance: "Why should I pay them to do things they should have to do anyway?" I can give you two reasons.

One: at least they'll have *some* notion of effort and reward. Most parents give their kids things and money without setting out *any* clear expectations of what the child must do in return. They buy them movie tickets, toys, snacks, CDs, expensive field trips, all with the expectation that somehow the child will appreciate these gifts so much that they'll be fighting over who gets to take the garbage out next time. Kids normally don't work that way. By giving them everything, you've led them to believe that life is a free ride.

Two: by giving them a set amount of money and cutting off the endless gifts and freebies, you're creating something more like real-life conditions for their first money experiences. Your child will be forced to manage the limited assets they've earned. While they're earning and learning, you can help them find ways to use their money more wisely. They can't just wait for the next handout and blow it on the first video game they see in a shop window. When it takes them time and effort to earn it, they will take more time and effort deciding how to spend it.

Sound familiar? Welcome to the real world.

Be sure that the child takes on specific age-appropriate responsibilities that earn them their weekly allowance. Write, or better yet, get them to write their job description. Every child, regardless of their age or limitations, can do some helpful things around the house.

Beth Moss has three-year-old Emily and five-year-old David pick up their toys, put dirty dishes in the dishwasher, set the table for dinner, feed the dog and help Mommy put groceries away. Beth posts a chart on the refrigerator at the beginning of each week. The chart lists the daily chores, and displays a row of boxes, one for each day of the week. Every time the kids complete a chore, Mom or Dad checks off a box. When all their work is completed at the end of the week, it's payday.

No work, no pay. Stand fast on this. I discourage parents from getting into partial payments if all the assigned jobs aren't done. You don't want to get into arguing with your kids about whether they get $2.56 or $3.23 that week. Remember, you're the boss and they're employees. They work to earn their paycheck; they're not entitled to anything if they don't fulfill their assigned responsibilities. An allowance is simply money provided to the child for being a working, contributing member of the family. Everybody contributes, and when they do, there's a reward.

If you have a particularly ambitious child, you can always let them earn extra money by doing extra jobs. Just like with the allowance, figure out exactly what the job entails and how much it's worth before they start work. Don't assume. Communicate about your and your child's expectations. This gives you and your kids a chance to discuss the relative value of different jobs. Do they get more for washing the huge SUV than the little sports car? Is it an hourly wage for big projects or a lump sum for the job? As with any contract, the more specific you can be with the details, the less chance for misunderstanding or confusion later. I've seen kids come up with pretty creative proposals for odd jobs to make more money.

Once your child is earning an allowance, it's time to help them determine what to do with their hard-earned bounty. This is where you'll decide how much of their loot they must save for later, and how much they can spend at their discretion. Is it part of your value system to give a regular amount to charity? You may end up dividing allowance money into three containers: a saving pot, a spending pot and a community pot. Be as creative as you like in choosing these containers.

Beth and Jake agreed that David and Emily would put aside 15 percent of their allowance in their savings bank and 10 percent in their community bank. This let's them keep 75 percent to spend on things they wanted or needed. David, their oldest, talked about saving up to buy a special bike he's had his eye on for some time. He spent his discretionary funds on games and toys. David used his community funds to tithe at his church every Sunday, just like his parents.

Emily on the other hand was the saver of the two. She enjoyed stashing every penny she made and liked listening to the sound of coins rattling around in her piggy bank. Besides giving her community bank money to adopt a whale, she rarely bought little trinkets or toys, preferring to save up and later splurge for the more expensive Barbie paraphernalia. She was thrilled to be able to carry her piggy bank to the Toys R' Us and cash in on her big purchases.

This simple process helps kids better understand the concept of budgeting, which can be simply explained as a plan that lays out what you're going to do with your money. Most kids, like many adults, don't readily embrace the idea of budgeting their earnings. It's hard to put off getting what we want. No matter how painful, budgets force us to pay attention to where our money is going. It disciplines the urge we all have for instant gratification. It makes us face the natural consequences of our financial choices.

As your child's money grows in the saving, spending, and community banks, it creates a great opportunity to talk about financial goals. Help them discover what's good about having goals. Make sure they're realistic: how long it might take to reach them? Is this a short term goal or a long term goal? Emphasize how good it feels to accomplish what they set out to do.

David and Emily thought long and hard before deciding to save for an expensive bike and some rather pricey doll accessories. They worked hard saving their money to get something they really wanted. Beth and Jake talked with them both about how proud they were for doing such a good job of saving their money.

At the same time, the children were learning how to spend their discretionary funds on smaller day-to-day purchases like trips with friends, gum, and the occasional small toy at the grocery store. Both big and small purchases had become a great opportunity for their parents to teach them about smart spending, comparative shopping, and how to portion out their money wisely.

I know this sounds like hard work. It's certainly easy for parents and kids alike to get tempted to abandon all this careful discipline. And believe me, retailers *want* us to fail! Commercial advertising targets children as never before, with the sole intent to create cravings that are difficult to ignore and impossible to satisfy. These days, companies spend over $3 billion annually on marketing directly to kids – more than 20 times the amount spent only a decade ago. Nearly half of U.S. parents say their kids ask for things by brand names by the age of five. But just because they've raised the stakes doesn't mean we have to take our eyes off the prize. Just think of those alluring ads as an opportunity to teach your kids about the dangers of reckless consumerism.

For young children, cash gifts from aunts, uncles, grandparents or friends require special thought and handling. Large chunks of money and lavish presents create a false economy, destroying the very values and lessons parents work so hard to instill. For example, if every time David and Emily are close to being able to cash in on their hard earned goals, Grandpa comes along and spends hundreds of dollars on a shopping spree for bikes, doll accessories, and an electric car, what's the point?

Parents have to stay in charge and help these gifts find their rightful place in the child's life. Small cash gifts, under $50 aren't a problem. Just divvy up the money under your regular allowance plan. Anything more than that goes straight to savings and/or the community jar. Handle any other windfalls, such as inheritances, the same way.

If a relative keeps foiling your efforts with frequent extravagant gifts, you'll need to call upon your diplomatic skills. Thank them for their generosity, but explain what you're doing and why. Most relatives don't want to do anything to intentionally hurt the children, and will temper their giving.

You and your children will encounter plenty of challenges to your financial curriculum, be they kindly grandparents or greedy retailers. But hang tough. Keep your eyes on the prize. You're helping your kids to acquire something that can't be bought in any store: *character.*

Beyond Money: Teaching Kids Essential Life Skills

All of the exercises, suggestions and directives you've encountered in this book have been aimed at a single goal: helping your children develop character, the primary ingredient in success and happiness. We've been concentrating on the financial aspects of character; now let's widen the focus.

Financial discipline makes a nice jumping-off point into several other realms of character. This is the best time for kids to pick up the habits of hard work, resilience, determination, self-control, zeal, and basic people-skills. They're at the perfect age to begin these lessons; their characters are still malleable, still forming.

"Our parents made us work for things from a young age," Jeff, the college-age son of millionaires Bob and Margie Anderson, once told me, "Sure, I griped about it at the time. What kid wants to do chores around the house? But as I got older I got used to it. By the time I turned eighteen, I had earned and saved enough money to buy my first car, and that felt *great!*"

Instead of a childhood stuffed with meaningless toys, which would by now be long forgotten, Jeff's parents gave him something that will serve him every day of his life: independence.

I used to think my parents were super-strict," Jeff's sister Jill told me, "While my friends kept getting all the new clothes, toys and stuff they wanted just by asking, our mom and dad would play this infuriating little game with us, asking us to distinguish between things we wanted and things we needed. As a kid, I hated it. Now I see why they did it."

Jill is mature beyond her nineteen years. She paid for her own college education out of pocket—she never had the desire, or the need, to ask her parents for tuition. "Besides keeping me out of financial trouble, their lessons have helped me deal with other situations that don't go my way. When I flunk a test or someone doesn't like me, I don't fall apart. I may get frustrated, but I get over it."

Jill's an old hand at not getting her way. Her parents gave her lots of opportunities to practice it.

Jack, Jill and Jeff's older brother, recalls a somewhat different experience: "I realize now that I was the guinea pig, being the first-born. I got away with murder for years, and they let me have whatever I wanted. It took them a while, but they finally started reining me in and making me work for the things I wanted."

Like all parents, Bob and Margie learned by trial and error. But they learned. They refused to take the easy way out. They stood firm and stayed involved. They got Jack turned around before he hit adolescence. Today he owns his own highly successful business, which he built from the ground up, without a single penny of his parents' millions.

Parents build the strongest foundations for their own families if they begin when the cement is still wet—when the children are first being formed and molded. But a late start is better than nothing. Let's look at what can be done with the adolescent who may have slipped into the storm of entitlement.

Chapter Ten:

From 13 to 18:
Braving The Storm of Adolescent Entitlement

Money was meant to be our servant.
But when we depend on servants too
much they gradually become our masters,
because we have surrendered to them
our ability to run our own lives.
—Phillip Slater

Jerry and Sue Perkins had finally had enough.

"I'm sick and tired of Stacy constantly nagging me about buying her things," Sue told me, "As a little girl it was always some new toy, but now it's big-ticket items. We've gotten her horses, jet skis, trips, designer clothes, computers, cell phones – last week she had to have a $2000 Cartier watch. It's never enough. Now she's whining that her friends at school get a new Mercedes on their sixteenth birthdays, so she's got to have one!"

"My son Steve's no better," Jerry complained, "He got drunk and wrecked the BMW I just bought him last month. Now he's mad that I haven't run out and picked up a new one yet!"

Ah, the sweet age of entitlement, when the heavens shift and the adolescent becomes the center of the universe. Our once sweet, innocent child becomes a feisty ball of wants, completely self-absorbed and demanding, exclusively focused on her own needs and desires. This difficult developmental stage is only further aggravated in those flourishing families with considerable means.

Fortunately, most adolescents outgrow this stage and mature into giving, responsible adults. Yet some become stuck in the quagmire of adolescent entitlement, expecting their parents to give them everything while they coast effortlessly from one indulgence to the next. In such cases, it may take a pretty stiff jolt to catapult these perpetual teens into adulthood.

Jerry and his wife Sue agreed that their kids had been spoiled rotten. They both felt it was time to do *something* about it, but they weren't sure what. Steve's recent drunken driving accident was the last straw. It was the incident that prompted our visit.

"We're not sure exactly how to change this pattern, but it has to change," Jerry insisted.

A true self-made man, Jerry had made a killing in real estate. Now in his fifties and partially retired, he continued to dabble in land deals while spending the rest of his time managing his multi-million-dollar portfolio. Sue was a homemaker who spent her spare time gardening and serving on community boards. Stacy, fifteen, and Steve, seventeen, both attended a top private school and, as Dad alluded, "wanted for nothing." The Perkins resided in a posh country club community where the children enjoyed all the amenities.

"When we were kids even having an old Chevrolet was a big deal. But in our house if it's not a Porsche or BMW, it's not special. They have this kind of monopoly money mentality – like its all a game. It's time we got off this roller coaster. I'm just no longer willing to support this kind of wretched extravagance," bellowed Jerry, becoming red faced as he spoke. "Where do these kids get this idea that we owe them?"

Jerry and Sue couldn't understand how they'd ended up with two obnoxious brats. Jerry had provided well for his family, as he had been raised to think that a good father should do. His business dealings had kept him away from home much of the time when the children were growing up. He left the responsibility of raising the children largely up to Sue. Sue's busy social life left her little time with the kids, either. The children grew up surrounded by pampering nannies and expensive luxuries. The entire family got caught up in a swirl of success and consumption, and lost sight of the bigger picture.

"We've created two monsters that, in a way, look a lot like we do. The only difference is they want what they want without having to earn it," Jerry said. "That's what really gets my goat. At least we earned what we have."

The more they examined their whirlwind lives, the more Jerry and Sue realized where they had gone wrong. "No wonder our kids are so spoiled!" Jerry fumed, "They've been given everything they've ever asked for, and they've never worked a day in their life. We've really dropped the ball on this one. But I'll be damned if we're going to keep making the same mistakes from here on out. We're going to take care of this right now."

He didn't yet realize what he was getting into.

I Never Promised You a B'mer: Dealing with Children's Great Expectations

When parents pamper and spoil their kids, they break the natural connection between effort and reward. These children feel they deserve to get what they want because of *who they are* and not *what they do*. Their sense of entitlement is inbred. As was the case with the Perkins' children, their feelings of entitlement are often the natural byproduct of too much generosity on the part of their parents.

As we've discussed, this disconnect between effort and reward occurs because parents don't feel like putting in the hard work to require effort on their children's part. Or, they're afraid of causing discord and bad feelings. The real irony is that the more children are given, the less they appreciate it. Instead, they want more and more. And the terrible cycle of entitlement continues.

In the Perkins family, Jerry had completely opted out of child rearing except to occasionally yell at them for their "laziness." To her credit, Sue had attempted at one point to institute chores and allowances.

But when the kids raised a fuss, or her schedule got in the way, she dropped the program. They reverted to their old pattern of giving the children whatever they wanted, while neglecting to give them what they needed.

Stacy and Steve's narcissistic entitlement was annoying to be sure. But if they carried this same set of behaviors just a few years into the future, they'd be looking at full-blown failure. Because the habits they had acquired in their privileged environment would never fly in the real world. If Stacy and Steve could not be helped out of their rut, they would be doomed to a life of dependent, self-centered adolescence.

No age betrays a privileged upbringing more than adolescence, though if not confronted, this attitude can continue right into adulthood. No matter what the child's age, entitlement is dangerous. It destroys motivation, breeds lethargy, lowers productivity, and in the long run crushes self-esteem.

When kids aren't expected to do anything, they don't! When adolescents aren't expected to grow up, and aren't given the tools they need to do so, they never get around to it.

The Perkins parents were ripe for change. Yet I still wanted to test Jerry and Sue's resolve to stick on the course they were setting. Were they prepared to hold fast, given that the children were sure to try to sabotage their efforts by using every emotional weapon at their disposal? Adolescents corner the market on anger, pity, guilt, and fear. Mom and Dad were talking about killing the goose that laid the golden eggs. Steve and Stacy weren't about to take that lying down.

We started by instituting the first Law of Financial Parenting: Jerry and Sue would now say no to things the kids wanted but didn't need. Stacy didn't need the Cartier watch or the Mercedes she asked for the previous week. Steve wasn't going to get a replacement BMW or the large flat screen TV he wanted for his room. Since he'd wrapped the car around a telephone pole, he'd be the one to come up with alternative transportation to school. For perhaps the first time in his life, Steve Perkins' actions had consequences.

Next, Jerry and Sue put Law #3 into effect. Now Stacy and Steve would have to do things around the house to earn their spending money.

"At first, they both laughed at the idea," Sue recalled, "But when they realized we were serious, they were mad as hell. Stacy actually cried. She was terrified of what all her friends would think of her."

"They dug in their heels and waited us out," Jerry told me, "They didn't think we would stick with it."

Jerry was absolutely right. They didn't have one ounce of credibility with their children. The kids knew from past experience that Mom and Dad had tried to establish chores and allowances before, but it never lasted. Why would this attempt be any different? Stacy and Steve fully anticipated in a few weeks that all this would be forgotten and everybody could get back to normal.

I warned Jerry and Sue that things would actually get worse once the kids realized they were serious. They did. The Perkins parents were suffering the painful consequences of playing catch up, of having been lax in their parenting for so many years.

Over the next several months, after much testing and bellyaching, Steve slowly began to adjust to the new reality. He eventually quit complaining about riding to school with his buddies and doing the few chores that were expected of him around the house. After depleting his small savings and mooching off his friends for a while, he found a part-time job working on Saturdays to earn some extra spending money. Steve was slowly learning that he had to work for what he earned and started showing more appreciation when his parents helped him out.

"Steve's coming around. We've agreed to help him with a new car but we're only to match what he saves to buy the next car. He's getting a real dose of reality and we're making him do all of the research on the kind of car he can afford. I can tell you it won't be a BMW," shared Jerry with obvious pride in his voice. "It makes me think back when I had to drive an old clunker – a 56 Oldsmobile. We called it Jezebel. I remember having to drive to school and park it next to a bunch of expensive cars. I got kidded a lot and it was definitely a humbling experience. Looking back, I see it was just those times that made me work so hard to get where I am. Maybe some of this will get Steve to work a little harder in school. He could sure use something to put some fire in his belly."

We dug deeper as the Perkins looked at the root causes of their family's problems. Jerry had come up the hard way; raised by his immigrant parents who'd worked hard all their lives, yet had never been able to escape their lower class lifestyle. "I remember being teased and picked on as a young kid because I didn't have nice clothes or the right car. I vowed to myself back then I'd be successful and never be in that position again."

From that decision, he never looked back. He ambitiously pursued the American Dream. His need to succeed at all costs was fueled by his own feelings of inadequacy, this inner insecurity driving his obsession with money and power.

We could see Jerry's compulsive pursuit of success as an addiction, something seemingly out of his conscious control. As Phillip Slater in *Wealth Addiction* states, when we start thinking of money as the main goal in life, "we begin to gradually believe that money is the key to the satisfaction of all needs. At that point, money ceases to be a tool and becomes our master. It distracts our attention from those desires that money can't satisfy and directs it toward those it does. For if we have money we tend to think of what it can buy – we forget about our own needs and goals and become shoppers and catalogue readers." In this regard wealth doesn't free us; it imprisons us.

As Jerry and Sue became increasingly wealthy they came to expect the deferential treatment often afforded the affluent. With some creeping false pride, the Perkins gradually succumbed to a mild form of snobbishness, expecting preferential treatment wherever they went. This attitude wasn't lost on their kids, who also learned to demand special, "better" treatment at shops, hotels, restaurants and other places they frequented. Their special treatment had to do with what they had, and nothing to do with who they really were. In many ways the kids had come by their sense of entitlement honestly.

Jerry suddenly found himself asking some tough questions. Have I lost my friends and family in my efforts to get ahead? How has my pursuit of money and possessions negatively affected my children and my relationships? Have I somehow transmitted my own narcissism to my kids? Have I lost any semblance of balance in my life? Like so many first time affluent, he had stumbled blindly into wealth, unaware of its dangers.

As happens with so many successful parents, the harder the parents work, the less the kids have to. Jerry and son Steve illustrated the classic "workaholic – bum" dichotomy. Jerry's over-commitment to work opened the door for Steve's lackadaisical, under-committed attitude toward life. Many underachievers like Steve hang out for years, fully expecting Dad's hard work and achievement to carry them through life. As long as Dad's carrying all of the load, why should I? After all, it'll all be mine some day.

Jerry and Sue began to understand some of the more subtle changes they could make to erase their kid's entitlement. Besides challenging their kids to earn their keep, they needed to look at their own expectations of "special" treatment – no more breaking in lines at the movie theater. Jerry saw how his working compulsively had left his own life out of balance and committed to develop a healthier attitude toward money and things, all with Sue's help.

It's hard to get kids, no matter what their age, to give up their demands and complacency. But adolescent entitlement is a particularly tough nut to crack. They naturally resist the hard lessons of accountability and responsibilities, preferring the warm comfort of the way things have been. Understand and expect this inevitable storminess on your journey, and determine to stay the course.

Confronting Entitlement: Helping Teens Learn to Earn

As we've discussed, many children of affluent families project an image of being "better than" the average person, often conveying a false bravado or snobbishness that alienates those around them. Yet the image these rich kids project may not at all be a true reflection of what lies within. Because they haven't had the emotional nurturing and limit setting that builds strong self-esteem, they're left to rely on externals to assure themselves and others that they're important.

Their self-worth is inextricably linked to money and materialism: fancy cars, expensive jewelry, designer clothing, prestigious schools, elite travel; they have allowed these externals to define them. Without these props, they are nothing. And even more than their parents, wealthy adolescents constantly compare themselves to their peers. What are my friends driving? What are they wearing? How much do their parents make?

These competitions are so prevalent because these things are so available to the rich. And quite simply, children want them. It's natural for parents to want to please their kids and give them what they want. It's much harder to say "no" and explain the reasons for our refusal. Adolescents can't help but feel they're being picked on, when the kid next door gets whatever she wants.

Be prepared. This is but one of the many weapons in a teen's arsenal. If you persist in "torturing" them this way, you'll be introduced to every manipulation tactic they've got.

Stacy was still fighting her parent's efforts to reign in her bratty behavior. Most of the time she pouted and stayed in her room. At first Stacy flatly refused to do anything around the house. She even taunted her brother when he helped out in the kitchen. But over time, when none of her antics changed her parent's position, she reluctantly gave in to the new order. Gradually she started doing more around the house. She took a part-time job in retail sales, something she had always believed was "beneath" her.

Jerry and Sue deserve a pat on the back. If they hadn't been willing to put in the hard work, to stand tough amid the fury of gale force whines, they would never have seen results. The only way to break the back of entitlement is to lean on it—hard! Parents must put relentless pressure on kids to make them earn what they get in life. But they must also practice what they preach, religiously. Children are much more likely to internalize these important lessons if they see their parents living them.

Teenagers can smell a hypocrite a mile away.

But let me tell you a potent little secret that will aid you in the battle to win back your child from the clutches of entitlement:

Most kids *know* when they're overindulged.

They'll never admit it to their parents. But they realize that they're getting away with murder. Psychologist Dan Kindlon, in his book *Too Much of a Good Thing*, reports that one of the most important findings that came out of his research on the Silver Spoon Syndrome was that kids recognize when their parents are too soft on them. Kindlon wisely cautions, "They know that in order to be strong, to face the challenges of life, to become the people they want to become, they need our help in building character, in fighting against the atmosphere of indulgence that comes part and parcel with living in the richest society the world has ever known."

But even knowing this, understanding it and dealing with it is still a fight. It takes time for children to accept that the entitlement is over. In fact, the longer the children were spoiled, the longer it takes for the change to set in. Parents must expect lots of whining, complaining, testing, fussing and other resisting. In fact, if you don't see some of this, you're likely not applying enough pressure.

But pressure and confrontation are only half of the equation; the other half is support.

Entitlement-busting isn't all about being tough. We also have to rebuild their distorted sense of self-worth. We have to show them that they are wonderfully unique, like all people. We must guide them, lovingly, to their true selves, and teach them that their real worth goes way beyond mere lineage and wealth. The most loving things we can do for our children, particularly when they're in the grips of the adolescence-monster, are to give of our time, and accept them just the way they are.

This is as important to the whole process as cutting off the flow of material goods. Your spoiled teen has gotten into the habit of thinking that money is what makes self-worth. Now that you've pulled the plug on the money machine, you've got to help them replace that false sense of worth with the real thing.

As they slowly grow out of the entitlement rut and make their way toward healthy adulthood, you'll see a brand new person emerging: confident, peaceful, at home in their own skin. It may take years, but eventually, your formerly entitlement-bound adolescent will discover that he *likes* earning what he gets.

Mature people prefer accountability; they want to work hard and be rewarded for their efforts. They enjoy being held responsible for their behavior and see their productivity count for something. People with an attitude of earning tend not to respect people who don't earn their success. Being held to task is the only way kids can learn problem solving, to set and accomplish goals, and to gain confidence and independence.

Emptying the Nest: Launching the Reluctant Teenager

Once the sense of entitlement is dismantled, it becomes easier for parents to set the stage for launching the young adult.

"I'm living with a 23 year old adolescent that can't keep a job and has dropped out of college. I believe he expects to stay here forever. At this rate, he'll be living here after I'm dead and gone," bemoaned one impatient father.

If the goal of raising children is to help them get out into successful lives of their own, then late adolescence is the launching pad. But parents hamper their child's autonomy by creating the kind of cozy nest that keeps them at home, discouraging them from developing greater responsibility and independence. For children to ever be happy and responsible, they must go out and succeed on their own.

George and Linda Carson came to see me about their daughter Andrea who, at the age of 20 was struggling to find a direction for her life after graduating from high school. Bright and personable, she'd focused most of her energies on socializing and showed only a passing interest in school. Consequently, she performed lukewarm academically.

Despite her parent's concerns and discussions, Andrea hadn't thought much about college. She'd taken a few classes at the local junior college, but she'd quickly lost interest and dropped out. She seemed content working part-time at the local gourmet shop as a cashier. Most of her free time was spent with friends, going to the beach and movies or just "hanging out."

As summer ended, Mom and Dad let her know she'd have to either work or attend college full-time to be able to stay at home. Having put off applying for college until it was too late, Andrea took a full-time position at the gourmet shop earning minimum wage. Her parent's were concerned she'd settled for working in what might inevitably be a dead-end job because she lacked the confidence to go away to college on her own.

"If something doesn't happen she'll be living at home until she's thirty!" Linda wailed.

I asked Linda if she thought Andrea might come and talk with me. A few weeks later I noticed Andrea's name on my morning schedule.

"My mom thought I needed to talk with you," Andrea announced the moment she entered my office, "I guess she's worried I don't have my head on straight or something. I don't know what I want to do with my life and I guess they see that as some big problem."

As we talked it quickly became evident Andrea was a sharp young woman with many positive attributes. Warm and engaging, it was clear she had highly developed social skills and would get along well with most people. She enjoyed working her cashier job and had no interest in returning to college or pursuing a higher paying job. When I inquired about her plans for the future she admitted she "hadn't really given it much thought."

"I know I can stay at home as long as I want so there's really no pressure to do anything. I'll never be able to live like this on my own, so why bother trying?"

Andrea was perfectly content right where she was. Why would she want to give up her cozy nest?

I only saw Andrea a few times before she dropped out of counseling. Fortunately she'd given me permission to speak with her parents about our visits, so I invited them in to discuss their concerns. I first assured them that fortunately there was no evidence of depression, learning disabilities, substance abuse or any of the other more serious problems that often detours the aspiring adult. Andrea's problem was more subtle, but just as insidious: a lack of motivation.

She was too comfortable depending on Mom and Dad. She had no reason to break free and make her own life. She was stalled on the launch pad.

Andrea wasn't spoiled; she didn't suffer from the ravages of narcissistic entitlement. She knew how to handle money. Her only problem was that she was a little too comfortably cocooned, sheltered from some of the world's practical, and at times, harsh realities.

No wonder she didn't feel that she could make it on her own.

That fall, I worked with George and Linda to develop a launch plan for Andrea.

Our goal was to help her take the small steps necessary to gain greater confidence and autonomy. As with any metamorphosis, we had to slowly strip away the protective layers of her cocoon while gradually introducing her to the world outside. Our goal became to help her experience successive approximations of the "scary" world she kept avoiding.

Andrea's parents let her know that she would be now given increasing responsibility for her living expenses, including clothing, personal items, car insurance and repairs, gas, spending money, pretty well everything except basic room and board.

Also she would be expected to be fully responsible for all her checking account and credit card expenses—no more help on these from Mom and Dad. They began charging Andrea $25 a week for rent, with the idea that it would increase over time.

"When it gets high enough," said Linda, "she'll figure out she might as well move out and get her own place."

No big surprise, Andrea wasn't excited about the changes. It quickly became apparent to her that her present income didn't come close to supporting her new expenses. All of a sudden she couldn't afford to buy new clothes and makeup, pick up CDs and trinkets, drive around town with her friends, or go out to eat as much. Her parents' worries, something she couldn't see as important, overnight became her own.

"How am I supposed to make it on what I earn?" she complained to her parents, "It's just not fair. You can afford to pay for this stuff. Why all of a sudden am I expected to support myself?"

Over the next few months it dawned on Andrea that there was less reason to stay at home. She had all the same expenses and responsibilities at home that she'd have on her own and more supervision than she wanted. Why not move out? After finding a roommate and scraping by for several months she returned to school, but this time armed with the determination to succeed and find a higher paying job. She had grown tired of living paycheck to paycheck. Going back to college became her idea. Andrea now knew that her life was truly her own.

Andrea's parents breathed a sigh of relief, and proclaimed their launch program a success.

Fortunately for George and Linda, Andrea found her wings after only one launch. But about 40% of slow-to-launch young adults return to the nest at least once. Whether they've lost their job, are hanging out after graduating college, have gotten a divorce, or just don't like the cold, cruel world, these "boomerang kids" will settle in for the long haul if you give them a chance. An awful lot of newly decorated guest rooms end up being converted back into full-time bedrooms. If your young adult crawls back into the nest, start making plans for the re-launch immediately!

First, discuss up front that the stay is temporary, and agree on a specific timeframe. If your child's stay ends up being open-ended, you're more likely to resent the disruption and the drain on your financial resources—not to mention the fact that the kid is wasting precious time that should be spent building his own life.

Second, their stay should involve a few conditions. They should be expected to follow house rules. Be sure the rules are explicit! If they're planning to stay more than a few weeks, make sure they understand work is involved, both at home and outside. Set a time by which they have to be employed, and once working, paying for room and board.

Be loving and firm, and treat your children like the adults you want them to be. If for some reason they won't follow these guidelines, make their visit brief. Work with them to make other living arrangements. And get them out.

As we safely sail beyond the adolescent storm of entitlement, we begin to glimpse the blue sky of young adulthood on the horizon. Let's focus on the special challenges parents face as their now-adult children encounter their first real taste of independence.

Chapter Eleven:

From 19 to 35:
Guiding the Young Adult to Achievement

No other technique for the conduct
of life attaches the individual so firmly
to reality as laying emphasis on work; for
his work at least gives him a secure place
in a portion of reality, in the human community.
—Sigmund Freud

"Casey's just barely making it in college," my client Jenny confessed of her wayward son, "Last year he was put on academic probation. He hides his grade reports and won't talk about how he's doing in school. We never see any books. We suspect he's just partying, like he did in high school. What can we do to break this pattern of laziness?"

Jenny's concern reflects a harsh reality for many parents. Just because they've launched their kids into jobs or college doesn't mean their work as parents is done. Now they face the next great parental challenge: helping their kids to achieve true independence in their young adult years.

Young adult children in their twenties are poised at a crossroads, often struggling to choose a direction for their lives. Developmentally, they face two primary challenges: first, they have to prepare themselves for the sphere of work through schooling or relevant vocational experiences. Second, and more importantly, they have to complete the tasks of finding their rightful place in the world.

Parents still have some influence at this stage, particularly in today's world where most young adults float along for several years in a state of extended adolescence. A rising number of adult children in their twenties, and even thirties, still depend on the parents financially. Some live at home, some receive money for college, and some count on their parents for large handouts to help cover their exorbitant living expenses, even though, supposedly, they're "on their own." Particularly in wealthy families, Mom and Dad are still in some way footing the bill.

These are critical years where following the immutable principles of financial parenting takes on even greater importance.

Ending Sloth: Breaking Patterns of Underachievement in Adult Children

Kids at any age need to feel worthwhile and productive. Meaningful accomplishment is one of the most critical components of positive mental health. As Thomas Edison said, "As a cure for worry, work is better than whiskey."

The value of work doesn't diminish just because a kid was born into an affluent family. The benefits of meaningful labor extend far beyond money. We need only listen to the emptiness and hollowness of the lives of many born to wealth to recognize that something vital is missing.

Studies have shown that when kids begin to develop their capacity to work while in their teens, they stand a much better chance of discovering a satisfying career later in life. Adults who held jobs as teenagers are far more likely to be satisfied with their lives in general.

The capacity to work is one of the most significant developmental milestones in the transition to adulthood. Its importance in an individual's life is on a par with mating and reproduction. Without meaningful work, children can never really grow up. In a real sense, work is a metaphor for true adulthood.

Children in their early twenties are usually preparing to assume the responsibilities of full-fledged adulthood, either through education or from early efforts at establishing a career. In either endeavor, I've seen a number of privileged children who find themselves stuck in a pattern of failure, unable to fully commit to, or succeed in, whatever they pursue. They may flunk out of college, languish in meaningless, low-paying part-time jobs, "hide out" in the family business, or squander their time in an endless cycle of half-cocked business ventures. Whatever the case, their young lives end up being nothing but a series of false starts.

These patterns of underachievement are a source of considerable frustration and distress, not only for the child, but for their families. Why can't John keep a job? What's keeping Chris from advancing in his company? How does Susan keep flunking out at three different colleges? When is Jimmy going to stop chasing after the "big score" with these crazy get-rich schemes?

In most cases, these children's failure to succeed has nothing whatsoever to do with their intellectual or creative abilities—and obviously it's not for lack of financial resources. Yet these bright, talented, economically advantaged young people just can't seem to get it together. Between their actual abilities and their concrete accomplishments stretches a yawning chasm, which they believe they are powerless to cross.

Jenny and Hank Reynolds called me to help them get to the bottom of their son Casey's problem. I had tested Casey a few years back. Given that he had knocked the top out of the intelligence scale, his parents couldn't fathom how such a bright kid could fail so miserably.

I could see the anguish on his parent's faces as they asked for help with their son. I was confident that given the right information, we could figure their problem out.

Fortunately, this kind of mystery is usually solved with a bit of psychological detective work. Underachievers perform poorly for a number of reasons: conflict with authority, rebellion against parental pressure, depression, fear of success or failure, low self-esteem, sibling conflicts, poor work habits, or a simple lack of desire.

As we talked more, the Reynolds gave no evidence suggesting their son was into drugs, although they suspected he was drinking too much. He was dating seriously and they'd grown to like his girlfriend who had on one occasion called Jenny worried about Casey's "down" moods and heavy partying. Until the last few months his parent's had taken a hands-off approach, hoping that he would sort things out for himself. But they hadn't stopped supporting him financially.

The three of us agreed to try to help Casey find a direction for his life.

Lost in Paradise: Knowing When You Should Push

It's often difficult for parents to know when to push and when to back off. It's a delicate balance: a complete lack of parental involvement can be just as destructive as riding kids to meet unreasonably high expectations.

But if your adult child is having trouble setting *any* realistic goals for his future, it's time to push.

Happiness often emanates from setting goals and working toward them. Goals provide direction and motivation—the antithesis of the aimlessness and lassitude we see in today's Spooners.

An occasional kid may discover goal-setting all on his own, but the vast majority of children must be *taught* how to set goals and work for them. The benefits of achieving meaningful goals are too vast to leave to chance. Parents need to be involved in helping their children set and reach goals.

Parents can have a tremendous influence on their children's ability to accomplish what they want in life. This influence often continues, subtly, even with older children like Casey. The Reynolds knew that they had backed off too far—they hadn't expected anything of Casey. Now, they knew it was time for a nudge.

It's a lot easier to teach goal setting throughout a child's growing-up years than it is to play catch-up with a directionless adult. Motivating young adults requires overcoming years of habitual sloth. It's not easy. But it can be done.

The Reynolds had to push Casey out of his comfort zone with a dose of tough love. They put an end to the monthly checks to cover his staggering beer tabs. In the new plan, they would cover only his basic monthly expenses; everything else would now be up to him. Then they demanded accountability: if he wanted his tuition bill covered next semester, he had to provide them with a grade report at the end of the term. A B average earned him another semester; anything less, and he was on his own.

For perhaps the first time in his life, Casey had a goal to achieve.

This was painful for the Reynolds to do. They feared that they were putting too much pressure on their already fragile son. They knew Casey would be unhappy, if not furious, with this new plan. But they firmly believed that their son would not overcome his inertia without a good, firm push.

Moms and dads frequently ask me whether I think kids should work part-time while they're going to college. I have one word for them: *Absolutely.*

When we talk about the benefits that their kids derive from working, parents agree enthusiastically that they want these things for their children.

Children need to be challenged. They must be stretched in order to grow. All the knowledge they're absorbing in those hallowed halls of academia won't mean a thing to them if they don't learn how to apply it. Work provides them with the skills they need to put all that good book-learning to use.

Unless your children are killing themselves just to make the grade, I think kids need to work in some capacity while they're in college. Whether this involves work-study positions, off campus stints, or summer jobs, a little labor never hurt anyone. One study conducted by Upromise, the Massachusetts-based administrator of college saving plans, found college students who hold part-time jobs perform better academically than those who don't work at all. Those 10 hours or so each week that they spent working cut into their non-productive activities, like TV watching. Of course, there is such a thing as too much work for college kids: the same study showed that students who worked full time were more likely to drop out.

Jenny and Hank made it clear that Casey would now have to work for his future; that they would only help him if he pulled his own weight. They knew any change wouldn't occur overnight. They were willing to stick to their guns until they saw a change in Casey.

It took several months, but Casey changed.

Some months later I noticed Jenny in my waiting area one morning, eager to talk. Once behind closed doors, she began, "Well, it's been bumpy but I think we're on the right course. Casey didn't make the grades so he's living at home and working. He hates it, but at least he's realizing we're not going to carry him anymore, and that without a degree, he's dead-ended. Now he's at least talking more about what he wants to do with his life. Hank decided not to let him work in our business until we see him make it first on his own. I wish we'd done all this sooner. We should have been more involved, and expected more from him all along."

Casey wasn't out of the woods yet by any stretch, but he was at least pointing in the right direction.

Negative Nudges: Can You Push Too Hard?

Parents sometimes make the opposite mistake: expecting too much. This is another reason some kids turn off. In the majority of cases in which I've been involved, affluent parents who pressure their kids too much run into just as many problems as those who ignore or coddle them. This kind of intense pressure usually comes from the overachieving, dominating parent who's been highly successful and then demands the same of their children. This usually sets the stage for a colossal control struggle.

These hard-driving heads of households expect their children to excel in everything they do: school, sports, music, art. They create a crippling pressure on their kids to attend the "right" schools, to look good, get the best grades and perfect test scores, get in the top universities, pick the most prestigious and powerful career, marry the "right" person from a socially acceptable family, to excel at any cost.

For some young people, the pressure's just too much. Trying to force children to live out our unmet dreams or to follow in our footsteps usually backfires, causing the child to either breakdown or perhaps in a more healthy response, rebel by underachieving. Kids who feel too much pressure shut down, sometimes purely to spite their overbearing parent. Believe me, you can't win this kind of parent-child power struggle. So don't try. If any of this seems familiar to you, back off and reevaluate your expectations.

Even for Adult Kids, Money Can't Replace Your Involvement

We all want our kids to reach their potential. The best we parents can do to help them on this journey is to stay involved, be encouraging and supportive, help them set and accomplish reasonable goals, and if problems present, set reasonable structure and consequences.

There are no shortcuts, no quick fixes. We can't buy this kind of support for our kids—in fact, that's where we went wrong in the first place! There is no substitute for parental involvement. Our kids require our time, our efforts, and our commitment.

Work on improving your relationship with your adult kids. Be available to them. Go to the school and talk with the teachers, get involved. Be sure you're not contributing to the problem by supporting the child's sloth and laziness, and if you are, stop by rearranging contingencies to encourage industry and effort. Make them work, in school or out. Over time, see if this helps.

If this fails, talk with a counselor. But don't give up. It just may be time to enroll your child in Hard Knock University.

The School of Hard Knocks: Lessons from the Real World

It's natural for us parents to want to share the good things in life with our children, and to want to protect them from pain. Challenges and setbacks are a necessary part of a full life, but wealthy kids are often cheated of these maturational experiences. Not only are they allowed to throw in the towel, their parents buy them a closet full of new ones!

But, as we've seen, by protecting them from adversity, failure, and pain, we deprive them of the opportunity to learn important lessons and coping skills needed to succeed in our highly competitive world.

Without these real world experiences, kid's can't develop a realistic sense of their strengths and limitations.

It's as if we're encouraging our kids to cheat in school—the school of life. We've talked about the way children's self-esteem can be undermined when they're never allowed to develop the ability to handle frustration and setbacks. Indeed, one of the hallmarks of what we call emotional maturity is the capacity not to be rolled over by life's inevitable obstacles: to be able to bounce back and persevere even in the face of adversity. How can a child mature if they're constantly sheltered from the very experiences so necessary for learning and growth?

Hard knocks help.

The school of hard knocks is the best place for our adult children's real-world education. Adversity is sometimes the best teacher. But how do we get them to enroll in Hard Knocks U and go to class?

Sometimes we have no choice but to cut them loose.

39-year-old Josh Adkins had enjoyed such a pampered, no-strings-attached existence that even as he approached middle adulthood, he was unable to function on his own.

His parents realized their mistake a bit late. "We've tried so hard over these years to make Josh's life easier than ours had been growing up," Josh's father Sam explained, "Beth and I never realized until now that all the help we gave him has created this big kid who can't take care of himself—let alone our business."

After much soul searching and some heated conflicts, Sam and Beth decided to sell the business and put Josh out on his own. They cringed at the thought of thrusting him out into the cold, cruel world, but they realized that it was their son's only chance.

"As hard as it is for us, its time we gave Josh an opportunity to make a life for himself," Sam told me, "We're taking the proceeds from the business and funding a charitable trust. We're leaving Josh just enough to get himself started. I've told him the gravy train had stopped and if he blows this money, there's no more coming. No more bailouts, no more gifts and rescue checks, no more midnight visits to the ER. His life's going to be exactly what he makes it."

Like many affluent parents, Sam and Beth had used their money to prevent their son's descent into the life-changing kind of "bottoming-out" experiences that are often necessary for change to occur. There is often great family pressure in the upper class to maintain a perfect facade, to never let on that there may be problems in paradise. Addictions, reckless habits, immoral behavior, even crimes may be smoothed over in an effort to protect the child from himself. Now, whenever Josh Adkins created a problem for himself, it would be staring him square in the face.

From now on, if Josh didn't like the consequences, *he'd have to change his actions.*

Affluent parents need to get out of the way for other reasons as well. Adult children need to know their true place in the world. When parents segregate their children, when they prevent them from participating in the world, they send the message that it's "dangerous" out there, that other people are inferior. Hearing this, kids begin to feel different, concluding that others are not their equals, or that these other people won't understand their special ways of thinking and behaving, or that others will be envious and try to take what they possess. Sometimes this type of elitism breeds prejudice, anxiety, and ultimately, isolation. Held back from mixing in everyday life situations, these privileged children develop one-dimensional thinking. They can't appreciate what is going on in the larger world.

Wealthy parents need to get out of the way of life's consequences. They need to pop the bubble of overprotection that is preventing their children from fully experiencing the outside world. This advice becomes even more important for the young adult who is just venturing out, where the parent's direct influence is already dwindling.

Let the world take over.

In letting go, parents must be willing to face that pain is a part of life—and often an essential condition for learning. After age 13, experience becomes the real instructor. The big lessons from that point on don't come from preaching, warnings, threats or stories, but from life itself.

Josh Adkins squandered the start-up money his parents had given him. In a few short years, he was destitute. He sometimes called his parents from homeless shelters, pleading piteously for help. He even did a little time in jail for petty larceny. After that, the Adkins didn't hear from their son for a while. They feared the worst, and began second-guessing their decision to cut Josh off.

Then one day, to their complete astonishment, Josh resurfaced. He was working days, installing air conditioners and heating systems. In the evenings, he volunteered at the rehab shelter where he had awakened on that fateful night when he finally hit bottom. He had a years' sobriety under his belt, and was sponsoring another young man in his struggle to remain sober. He admitted he'd been furious with them for a long time. But now things were beginning to look different to him. Josh realized that, at thirty-two, he still had a lot of catching up to do. His life was still only a shadow of what it could have been, but for that he now blamed himself more than he blamed his parents.

Josh confessed that he still wasn't ready to resume a full relationship with them. But he ended the conversation with the promise to stay in touch. He asked for their prayers, but not for their money.

An adult at last, he would never again allow them to protect him from his own life.

Josh' parents had suffered horribly from their decision to cut their "aging child" loose. Many a time, they wondered whether their son might have eventually pulled himself together without such drastic measures. But a glance at the annals of America's wealthiest families reveals that such children seldom do so on their own.

When Ned McClean, the second generation to own the *Washington Post* lost the paper in 1932 to Eugene Meyer, no one was surprised. Having a reputation for a "weak character," Ned had never been obliged to pass through any of the ordeals that the school of hard knocks curriculum prescribes. On the contrary, his parents had gone out of their way to spare him all that.

Ned was the poster child for pampered progeny. His mother used to bribe his playmates to let him win at Parcheesi. His father, hearing he was at home with a cold once sent him a note, "Tell Pop the truth, how are you? Everything is going to be all right here at the *Post*. All you have to do in the world is stay well. Pop will take all the responsibility, I am holding the *Post* for you."

Ned became an alcoholic and fell victim to "urination syndrome," an unfortunate affliction he shared with another newspaper heir, the New York *Herald's* James Gordon Bennett, which compels its victims to pee in open fireplaces, ladies reticules, potted plants, any convenient place so long as it is in public view. Not unexpectedly, he squandered his kingdom as well. It took him sixteen short years to plunge the *Post* into ruin.

Children who've been given lots of love and limits and have graduated from the school of hard knocks stand a much better chance of becoming happy, productive citizens of the community. But to fully complete this journey, they must also find a labor to love. This is an essential developmental task facing every young adult.

The Good Career Fit: Helping Them Find a Labor to Love

It's one of the most difficult tasks for any young adult: to decide what to do, to figure out a direction for their lives. What we do for a living largely influences our income, social status, choice of friends, even our core identity. People who are unhappy in their work are generally unhappy in their life.

Our occupation is our primary way of defining ourselves. This is not new; Ralph Waldo Emerson wrote in an 1860 essay on wealth, "As soon as a stranger is introduced into any company, one of the first questions which all wish to have answered is, How does that man get his living. He is no whole man until he knows how to earn a blameless livelihood."

Think how often your social introductions are peppered with the question, "What do you do for a living?"

Selecting the right career, like finding the right mate, is a complex, often confounding process. Both endeavors usually involve a lot of trial and error, and often a lot of costly mistakes. Those fortunate enough to make a good occupational match stand to reap considerable psychological as well as financial benefits, for it is these same fortunate people who are most likely to be deemed successful in life.

I've done career evaluations and counseling for years. In helping people to "find their bliss," I've discovered that good career "fits" require three essential ingredients:

the right interest
the right abilities
the right personality.

If you're missing any one of these key ingredients, the cake falls flat.

Obviously, when we're interested in an activity, we enjoy doing it. We get excited at the prospect of tackling the activity's particular problems. If you prefer the outdoors, a desk job is likely to stifle you. If you hate numbers, you won't be happy going through life as an accountant.

But interest is not enough. We must be able to do the activity well. There is such a thing as talent, and in some fields, it can make or break our ability to participate. What are your daughter's talents, her core strengths? Is your son a math or business whiz, an artistic genius, a social charmer or a science wizard? Everyone has a set of unique aptitudes and abilities waiting to be discovered and applied.

Personality refers to those enduring characteristics that define who we are and how we relate to the world. Some individuals possess a strong inclination toward leadership; others shrink from it. Some careers call for an aggressive personality; others for an easygoing one.

All three factors are necessary to a good career fit. If any one of these is missing, career dissatisfaction and disillusionment aren't far behind. You may have a wonderful operatic voice, a musical talent that could bring down the house and a diva's sparkling personality to boot. But if you have absolutely no interest in music, you're not likely to become a world-class tenor.

So when's the best time to tackle the career question? Obviously, the earlier our children begin thinking about it, the better, although young adulthood is the first real opportunity to get reliable answers to these questions. Many of our interests, abilities and much of our personality are still developing throughout adolescence and into early adulthood.

If your kids haven't figured out what they want to do by the time they hit their late twenties, it's time to worry. But being concerned doesn't mean you hand them a job in the family business, or write a blank check for their support. Let them work it out themselves.

Stand back financially; stand in emotionally. Be supportive, but don't take control.

Parents can get in the way of good career choices, sometimes by their overzealous efforts to "help." They may give heavy-handed advice, they might pressure the child to take over the family business, or they may be too willing to bankroll their latest venture. The urge to maintain this level of influence comes from an inordinate desire for control. But, though they may lend support, parents cannot choose their child's path in life.

Wise parents resist this urge to control. They allow their children maximum freedom in their choice of career. Some children will feel an intense need for autonomy while others will not. Whatever their age and bent, most kids respond far better to encouragement, combined with a sense of personal choice, than they do to parental pressure.

The Darker Side of Green: Dodging Wealth's Shadow

There's no question that wealth brings tremendous career advantages. Affluent parents can buy their offspring the best education. It's easier to market, network, and open doors when you're well heeled and have the right connections.

Yet it's not all a bed or roses. Kids of high net worth parents face unique career obstacles. Those who inherit great fortunes, or high positions in the family business, are often left with a gnawing sense of inner doubt, wondering if they could have ever made it on their own. It's particularly hard for young beneficiaries to bank the kind of achievements that build strong self-esteem. In their case, most of the hard work, sacrifice, and ability were the prior generation's, not theirs. No matter how hard they work, their accomplishments are often overshadowed.

Even significant achievements can feel like failures. Their successes only reinforce the suspicion that their money, or their parent's money, made them easier. No matter what their accomplishments, their wealth always seems to taint their success.

One young inheritor consulted me over this common lament, "Everybody's always felt that I've done well because my family had money. Everyone assumes they bought my way into the best schools, and later, they "bought" me good jobs. They assume that my parents somehow arranged everything good that happens to me, that my whole life's been fixed. No matter how hard I work or what I accomplish, it's somehow discounted. It's been terribly demoralizing. Even now in my late 20's, I feel like giving up."

In order to feel successful, these heirs find that they must surpass the accomplishments of the previous generation. Yet even if they double the size of the family business, or turn $10 million in assets into $40 million, nobody gives them credit, because of where they started:

"Hell, who couldn't do that with a $10 million dollar pot to start with!" There's always the nagging suspicion that their lucky birthright provided the push that made their success a downhill ride.

How do wealthy children deal with these hazards? A lot of rich kids, particularly those offspring of highly successful business tycoons, make a point of entering the professions or the arts. There, their competence and success can't be attributed to the size of their inheritance. This is one way to escape wealth's shadow.

The late James Merrill, an accomplished poet and son of Charles Merrill of Merrill Lynch, escaped the negative influences of his father's wealth via this route. James wrote poetry from an early age. His father encouraged him to pursue a career in writing. James soon became an acclaimed poet in his own right, though his success was tinged with conflict. He said of this struggle, "People thought I must have paid to get my poems published, which used to bother me. I felt I had to struggle even a bit harder than other writers just to prove myself. I suppose I was eager to achieve something of my own, but I don't worry about that anymore."

Similarly, Peter Buffet, son of billionaire Warren Buffet, doesn't mind that his father intends to leave him little upon his death. He's determined to make his fortune on his own. He has already turned a $2,000 inheritance from his grandfather into several hundred thousand dollars. He used this money to purchase sound equipment and is now pursuing a successful music career.

Warren Buffet has encouraged his son all along to go it on his own. He's acutely aware of the immense price his son would pay in motivation and self-esteem if his financial success had simply been handed to him on a platinum platter.

Unfortunately, in my research on the super-wealthy, I discovered few parents with that much insight and discipline.

Both James Merrill and Peter Buffet had fathers who supported and encouraged them to stand on their own, to take risks, and to make their own choices. To their credit they were also wise enough to choose artistic careers that require talent—something money can't buy. Interestingly, Peter Buffet is convinced that he would not have worked nearly as hard as he has, nor be as successful in his career, if he had been assured of inheriting his father's money.

Another way benefactors try to overcome wealth's shadow is to become benefactors themselves. They support charities, libraries, symphonies, hospitals, museums or other worthy causes. They're esteemed according to their generosity, which in itself can be a precarious foundation upon which to build one's self-worth. If for some reason they withdraw their support, they may quickly find themselves pariahs among the very same group that revered them just a short time earlier. For this reason, rich kids seldom find philanthropy alone to be satisfying.

If productive work is the pivot around which America revolves, it must follow that not to work is, in a way, to be irrelevant. The psychological difficulties inheritors face in finding a legitimate social function are very real. Michael Stone, a psychiatrist who has worked for years with children of the rich says, "If one is not constrained to labor, one is not constrained to accomplish. It is therefore rare for anyone of great inherited wealth to do first-rate creative work, and often they cannot orient themselves toward any life of accomplishment."

Nelson Aldrich approaches this existential dilemma of the wealthy somewhat differently in his book, *Old Money*. The inheritor, Aldrich claims, is confronted every day with the choice of doing nothing, of inaction. It's a choice that almost no one else has, he contends, and it turns the rich into a class apart. He offers, "Not to make these choices, not to open oneself to misfortune and the fear of misfortune, is a tempting option, but one gives into it at a risk of never living a fully human life...they do not connect, they do not engage, they do not possess the richness and complexity of experience."

Many of us get caught up in the stereotypical trust fund loafer or troublemaker, the trustafarian who is caught up in squandering their good fortune on parties, expensive cars, jewelry and drugs. But we often fail to see those children who take even more drastic, though subtle, measures to free themselves of its shadow. They become tired of the strain, worry, guilt and headaches created by their money.

When people open up to me, it's often because they feel there's no one else to talk to about the more personal side of money matters.

Some of those who come to me are so haunted by their wealth that they are seriously considering giving it all away. As strange as it may sound, they yearn for what they don't have, a simple life without all the complications their wealth has brought them. They want to be a person, not a person "with 10 million dollars."

Some of these desperate inheritors *do* decide to repudiate their wealth. Their radical approach to ridding themselves of their inheritance is called zeroing-down.

These children cope with their inherited wealth by divesting themselves of their riches so that they can prove – to themselves and others – that they can make it on their own.

Chuck Collins is one such "down to zero," as he calls those who give away their inheritance. Collins, the grandson of the founder of Oscar Meyer, grew up in the affluent neighborhood of Bloomfield Hills.

"I remember the Detroit riots, feeling even as a kid, a sort of cognitive dissonance when I looked at the burned out parts of the city and thought about the nice area where we lived," Chuck wrote, "I didn't think it was fair that a lottery of birth should give people privileges, and I didn't even think my trust fund was 'my' money. The Oscar Meyer workers and my family had created that value, and there were others who needed it more than I."

Zeroing-down isn't easy. Collins explains his struggle, "At age 25 I came into control of my trust, about $350,000. For two years I thought about how I could divest myself of the money without making my family think I was rejecting them. I also met two other people who wanted to divest. We called ourselves The Class Suicide Support Group and started meeting to think through what we wanted to do."

Chuck Collins traded his trust fund for a shared house and car. "It took me a year and a half to disburse all my funds, and I did feel different afterwards. I felt I had aligned my personal life with my values. Also, I learned for the first time to live more simply, within a budget, and I found I took pleasure in that. Today I rely on other people more – which was scary at first. The rich just sail over life's traffic jams, but I can't do that anymore."

These brave zero-downers' journal of self-discovery tells us much of what all human beings need and how they should be raised. They tell us by their struggles that the search for purpose and meaning in this life is not a treasure hunt.

As we've seen, children of fortune, though in some ways advantaged, also face distinct obstacles in their search for a labor to love. Parents need to be cognizant of how their money and influence can both help and harm their child's efforts to find their place in the world.

In the next chapter, we'll examine the transference of wealth in greater detail. We'll discuss the importance of timing in handing over the reins of the family fortune, and we'll outline a strategy for counteracting many of the common hazards of inheritance.

Chapter Twelve:

From 36 to 55:
Loosening the Reins
in the Middle Adult Years

*The lust for comfort, that stealthy thing
that enters the house as a guest and
then becomes a host and then a master.*
—Joseph Conrad

"Dustin's in his early-thirties and still living the high life," said Henry Sloan, a wealthy businessman torn apart over what to leave his three children, "He's played hooky from college and has never held onto a job for more than a few months. I think he works seasonally as a ski instructor, but that's it. He's spent most of his time playing around. He's never settled down, never accomplished anything worthwhile in his life.

"Jack, his younger brother, is in worse shape. From what I hear he hasn't worked in years. He just hangs out with his buddies and gets loaded. If it wasn't for some money we've given them, I don't think either of them could make it," Henry sighed, his heart near breaking, "Their mom and I have some tough decisions to make as we figure out an estate plan."

Henry and his wife are like millions of other parents caught on the horns of a dilemma. How do they pass on their wealth in ways that are best for their children?

I've faced these questions in my own life. My generation of Baby Boomers, those 74 million folks born between 1946 and 1964 who are now somewhere between the ages of 37 and 54, have been dubbed the "The Inheritance Generation." Economists Robert Avery and Michael Randall report that over the next 50 years my generation would inherit around $10 trillion dollars. In the last five years alone, Boomers have received 2.4 million bequests, totaling more than $365.7 billion dollars. And that's just the beginning. Over the next few decades, millions more will become instantly wealthy through inheritance.

They'd better keep their wits about them. For a particularly nasty class of demons lurks nearby whenever wealth changes hands.

No matter when or what the size of the estate, all affluent parents must decide at some point the safest, fairest, most constructive way to divvy up their assets. When's the best time to make distributions? How should the money be transferred so as not to disrupt their child's life? How best to handle the transfer of a family-owned business? Can we encourage better behavior in our kids by the way we distribute assets? How much inheritance is too much? We'll address each of these critical questions in turn.

Lessons Learned, Lessons Lost: Kids Set in Their Paths

Let's face it. If your adult children haven't learned to be become responsible, decent human beings by the time they've reached their late thirties, it's probably not going to happen. As sad as this may be, parents at some point have to face reality if they have any hope of salvaging what they can. By this time, you have to accept that whatever lessons you've tried to teach over the years have either been learned or lost. By the middle adult years your children have set their course in life.

If they're going to have a family they've already started, or are at least laying the foundation for one. If they're going to work productively, they've gotten through school and are well on their way to a stable and hopefully meaningful career. If they plan to make a contribution, to their family, their community, or themselves, they are already seeing some of the psychological or economic payoffs of their contribution.

Or not. Unfortunately some adults are perennial children. They may still manifest many of the signs of Silver Spooners. These people act much younger than their chronological age. Though physically mature and legally adults, they're psychologically adolescents at best. As we've seen, these Spooners are financially irresponsible, have unstable work histories, and are often economically dependent on their parents. Shallowness and manipulation frequently mar their relationships as they languish in a developmental flux, never quite growing up.

We've all heard the tragic tales of children ruined by their riches. Millionaire Christina Onassis, whose inheritance kicked out a yearly stipend of $50 million dollars died of a heart attack at thirty-seven, likely caused by drug abuse. Jon Winokur in his book, *The Rich Are Different,* quotes one of Christina's best friends, "Ms. Onassis had a pathetically wasted life! With all of her millions, she did absolutely no good for anyone—especially herself. Where were the foundations, the good works, attempts to help the poor, hungry and homeless of the world? No, for her it was a tour of the road of self-indulgence. Obsessive sex, consoling herself with $300 bottles of Diet Pepsi (flown in by private jet to her remote hideaways) and all the rest." Every wealthy parent's nightmare!

Even though they weren't the Onassis's, the Sloans had worries of their own. Henry and Sandy saw that their kids were completely irresponsible, in direct contrast to their hard-working, frugal parents. The Sloans, like many affluent couples, were not ostentatious. They did not live on a scale that belied their great wealth. They were part of the closet wealthy, having hidden their true net worth in order to escape the social isolation and envy often visited on the rich.

Most of the rich I've dealt with are really lovely people, largely unaffected by their wealth. Like the Sloans, they consider themselves blessed, and are humble about their success. They worked hard and view their money as a byproduct of their industry, not an end in itself. They live modestly; the quality of their lives is defined more by people than by possessions. Conscientious parents, the Sloans had agonized over what they could do with their fortune to enrich their kids' lives.

"We've tried to send the right messages to the kids growing up," said Henry, "I don't know where we went wrong. Two of our kids are bums. It's caused us to have some late night discussions, and at least a few arguments," Henry offered, turning to smile wryly at his wife.

Like many parents, they had given their children money to get started in life. The Sloans, however, had taken their generosity to the extreme. It had started with toys, clothes, and computers, and had become a complete subsidy of their children's lives, from houses and vacations to cars and credit cards.

When they gave each of the three kids three-quarter million dollars on their eighteenth birthdays, they had not thought of the way this sudden windfall might affect them in the future. Henry and Sandy fully believed that all they were doing was helping their kids to be happy. But when their children hit their late twenties and early thirties, the Sloan parents saw what their money had done. And they didn't like what they saw.

"Our wealth," Henry continued, "started out as a blessing, Dr. Buffone, but it's ended up a curse. Our intention was to do good for our kids but instead they've become parasites. We expected our kids would go on to college and find careers and families. They both keep promising us that next year they'll go back and finish. Jack's been going to a two-year community college for the past six years. These boys wouldn't know work if it bit them in the butt. The only thing they've stuck with over the past several years is the local happy hours at the bars," Henry added bitterly.

Sandy nodded in agreement, "They've built their whole adult lives around what we've given them, and on the inheritance they know is coming. They're like vultures, waiting for us to die."

The Sloans' tale confirms what all parents know in their heart of hearts: money not earned is no gift. When parents give their kids a blank check, what reason do they have to get off their duffs? Or as Ross Perot once said, "If your kids grow up living in fairyland thinking that they're princes and princesses, you're going to curse their lives."

Whichever road your children have chosen, at this point they're well down life's path. This is the time for parents to make their best decisions about passing on their wealth. As we move forward, you'll notice that I'll be focusing less on developing character, as we did with the younger child, and more on influencing the adult child.

That's all parents can do with adult children: hope they can offer a positive influence.

Parents transfer wealth in two ways: either by letting their kids take over the family business or through outright cash gifts and inheritance. We'll look at both of these, but let's start with a few words of caution.

Sharing the Wealth: Timing Isn't Everything

Many wealthy parents have discovered that it's harder to give away money than it was to make it. Figuring out the details of wealth transfers can be a huge headache. Few people enjoy the endless meetings with professionals, the complicated legal and accounting principles, the minutiae of probate, and the painstaking process of cataloging all the possessions.

And that's just the *impersonal* side of inheritances.

This painstaking process of wealth transfer is yet another essential part of financial parenting. As I've witnessed many times, the heads of affluent families find out, often too late, the disastrous consequences of poorly planned financial gifts to their children.

We've all heard the nightmarish stories of families ripped apart by money. Parents can't figure out what went wrong. What could have happened to cause close siblings to stop talking to each other, for children to cut themselves off from their parents, or for parents to disinherit their grandchildren? How can heads of households plan their disbursements to prevent—or at least minimize—the kinds of familial catastrophes that often befall the moneyed?

As hard as it may be to believe, a number of affluent parents don't fully consider the emotional consequences of these very weighty decisions. These aren't the kinds of issues people usually discuss with tax attorneys or accountants. A financial advisor can't answer these tough personal questions. They can only be answered by taking a hard look at yourself, your values, what you want most for your children, what role sentiment plays in your life, how you wish to live in your later years, and the legacy you wish to leave behind. When it comes to these deeply personal questions, you're better off seeking out a trusted priest or therapist, a wise friend or uncle, than consulting a lawyer.

I've served as a confidant and advisor on these types of questions for nearly two decades. Let me share with you some of the things I've learned about this delicate topic.

When is Right? Answering The Timing Question

Parents make several common mistakes in this difficult transition, the most frequent one being the bestowal of wealth before the child is psychologically ready. As I've mentioned, adult children need to have time to find themselves and carve out their niche in life before they're ready to take on the additional responsibility of wealth. I believe the timing of large gifts and inheritances is a critical factor, even more important than how much money is given.

This was part of Henry and Sandy Sloan's mistake. Besides giving too much and expecting too little from their sons, they dropped large wads of cash on the boys the minute they hit 18. Right at that point, from that one decision, the damage was done. The sizeable gift had effectively killed any motivation for the two of them to ever work again.

I suggest parents wait until their children are in their mid-thirties before transferring control of major assets. By this age, children have had time to establish their families and careers, and have probably reached the peak of their emotional maturity.

Or not. The fact is, if they haven't by this age, they probably never will. In which case, plan accordingly. Clearly, if you have a child who has never made it, never become responsible, and never established a stable life structure, at least you can make decisions based on that fact.

I suggest you keep your money in trust at least until your kids are in their mid to late thirties. This way, you have control until you make up your mind about what you want to do. If your kids are doing well, you can let them have the money when they reach the age stipulated in their trust. If you have one or more children proving to be a derelict or a spendthrift, you can decide if you want them to have the money anyway, or if you want it to stay in trust for good after you're gone.

As a rule of thumb, if you're really uneasy about the way your kids might handle such a transfer, adopt a "wait and see" approach.

Sometimes children of rich families resent the fact that they have to make it on their own, knowing that their parents are sitting on a goldmine. A son struggling to make ends meet will growl to his wife, "I can't believe how hard I have to work when a few hundred thousand would really make our life easier. It's not as if Mom and Dad couldn't help – they've got millions." This situation may not promote harmony in a parent-child relationship, but that's because Junior can't see right now the fact that you're protecting his incentive to succeed. Some day, he may thank you for it.

I suggest parents hold their ground when they encounter this kind of resentment. In fact, the more pressure you're getting from your kids to gift them, the more reason you need to be cautious. But if you absolutely must give in, consider a middle ground where you offer a more moderated enrichment, make the gifts small, and only after the children have clearly established themselves independently.

If at all possible, wait longer before bestowing major gifts. Age is certainly an influence in the way we relate to money. The older we get, particularly once we hit our fifties, the less we care about acquiring material things. Most people's consumerism wanes as new expressions of wealth become more and more modest. If you can wait, hold off on transferring monetary assets until your kids are well into middle age. This way, the money comes at a time when most people no longer have the desire to do anything crazy with it.

The timing of your gift is important. But it isn't everything. In the end, your material legacy, however well you time it, will not be nearly as important to your kids as the gift of *yourself*.

Enriching the Kids: Is It Love or Is It Just Money?

Parents also frequently make the mistake of confusing love with money. Children of wealthy families often tell painful stories of parents who gave them everything except themselves, a style of parenting I refer to as "generous neglect". Instead of giving of their time, these parents gave things, instead of offering caring, they gave cash, instead of providing attention, the parents offered alms.

Money becomes, in many affluent families, a substitute for love. The results of this substitute are all too often apparent in the enormous amount of dysfunctional behavior within the so-called privileged class. This money-for-love trade off is at the root of the Silver Spoon Syndrome.

Parents often do this out of guilt. Instead of providing nurturing, they wrote a check. They are trying, consciously or unconsciously, to make up for years of absence and emotional neglect. Remember Granny, who dropped millions of dollars in her grandchildren's laps to show them how much she loved them? Somehow these parents believe they can purchase love, just like they've purchased so many other things.

Don't make this same mistake when considering your children's inheritance. Don't confuse love with money. If you have to choose to give one or the other, give love, and keep your money.

Painful Procrastination: Recognizing The Myth of Tomorrow

Parents also frequently make the blunder of procrastination when it comes to their estates. Somehow, they manage to put off making these difficult decisions until the worst possible times. As I've pointed out in my book, *The Myth of Tomorrow*, people very often defer what they don't want to face, namely, their mortality, and this persistent denial frequently brings with it devastating consequences.

Unfortunately, sometimes tomorrow never comes: the parents die or are incapacitated and the surviving family members are left frantically scrambling, trying to make sense of and settle what are often rather complex estates.

Studies conducted by psychologists over the past two decades point to the disastrous consequences of making critical decisions while in the midst of an emotional crisis. After a sudden loss, grief can hit like a sucker punch. Family members are dazed, confused, and frequently in the throes of an emotional tornado that can lead anyone to mismanage an inheritance. Grief-stricken and depressed, they need time to heal from their loss, not push through the financial maze of settling an estate.

"I had no idea where my parents were financially, they would never talk about it," shared Beth, a sudden inheritor of a large and rather messy estate. The oldest of four children and surprise executor, she was left to sift through the complexities of their sizable assets while in the midst of a disabling grief. As so many in her position, Beth felt lost and vulnerable, subject to pressure from other people, particularly family members, to make decisions that they could all later regret.

I, and every financial advisor, will tell you the same thing, be proactive and plan ahead. Be thoughtful and spare your loved ones this agony by handling your estate planning *now*, when you're at your best. As painful as it may be, the best time to figure out the complicated and emotionally laden questions on the disbursement of wealth is now.

Believe me when I tell you that one of the greatest gifts parents can give their kids is a well considered and organized estate plan. For some sound advice on this topic talk with your advisors and see Michael Alexander's *How to Inherit: A Guide to Making Sound Financial Decisions After Losing a Loved One.*

Knotted Purse Strings: Let's Be Reasonable

In a bid for better behavior, parents occasionally attempt to give their children money or gifts tied to a host of unreasonable conditions. They just can't quite let go of the economic reins. We've all heard the stories of the tyrannical father who made the kids inheritance contingent upon their marrying a certain spouse, or choosing a particular career, or their keeping the grandchildren within a certain geographic area. Some parents bind their children with silver strings long after their deaths, virtually extending their control from the grave.

Some would say gifts are gifts and no conditions should apply. That may be true in some circumstances, but I do think there are certain times when it is correct to set conditions on a child's inheritance. We'll discuss these in the next chapter, which is all about estate planning instruments and trusts.

When Blood and Business Mix: Passing On the Dream

This next section is specifically for those parents, many of who began as entrepreneurs, whose primary assets are now wrapped up in a family-owned business. Whether you're the founder, the owner's spouse, or one of the second-generation, you face the special challenges that arise when blood and business mix.

Substantial wealth in this country exists within family businesses, the backbone of the American economy. Most people don't realize that nearly 90% of businesses in this country are family owned. Unfortunately many business-owning parents do a poor job of effectively planning for succession, largely because the stakes are high and issues volatile. Therefore it's not surprising that fewer than a third of family businesses survive into the second generation and well less than a fifth make it into a third generation. That's why you sometimes hear the old saying, "The third generation always closes the business."

Examples abound of wealthy parents who expect their sons to take over the family business, with little regard for the interests or talents of the child, and exaggerated concern for the expectations and traditions of the founder. Recall the dilemma the Adkins parents faced. They worried that their son Josh wouldn't have what it would take to keep their family business afloat.

Business successions raise all kinds of other thorny questions. Is the founder prepared to relinquish control of the company? Are the parents ready for retirement, and is their future income independent of the success of the business? Can the business survive without the owner? Should the successor come from outside the family? Has the successor been properly prepared to take over? Is succession really what's best for this particular child?

Despite these challenges, many parents often want to pass the business to the next generation. They make this decision not only because they've worked hard to create it and crave the satisfaction of seeing it support their descendants, but also because they feel an understandable desire to leave a legacy.

Parents generally assume that their kids *want* to take over the family business. Often they're correct. But even though a child is eager to

146

fill his parent's shoes, he may not be the best candidate for that particular pair of footwear. Everyone wants to live on the top of the mountain, but few understand that true happiness and growth comes from climbing it. Some children figure the business is their birthright, that they're entitled to it because of their blood relationship with the founder. But a head for business doesn't always transfer with the genes.

Sam, the son of one of my clients, figured he deserved to take over his father's industrial supply business simply because he'd been born next in the line of succession. Sam had been given a job in the company right out of high school, but he had never taken it seriously. He habitually showed up late, if he bothered to show up at all. He focused more on flirting with the office staff than on his work as a sales coordinator. Fortunately his underling picked up most of the slack, a fact not lost on his father.

"I'm going to let Sam go," said Sam Sr., "He's never worked at his job. People around here resent his laziness and his bad attitude. I don't like it that he's tried to take advantage of his family ties. Hell, I feel more like his meal ticket than his father. The only time I see him is when he wants something from me."

Sam Sr. resented his son's expectation that the business was his simply because he stood next in line. Even though Sam Sr. wanted his son to succeed him, the father realized that Sam hadn't developed the necessary maturity to take over. Only the wisest of parents carefully considers whether or not their children are truly right for the job.

Transfers of family businesses are fraught with pitfalls. The fact that professional colleagues are also family members creates a breeding ground for strife. We've all heard the horror stories: the over-controlling patriarch who won't let his son make the smallest decision, the smoldering resentment of the brother who works two jobs to carry the sibling who won't work one, the parents who demand that their children show up for Sunday dinners to get their paychecks, the daughters assigned jobs as bookkeepers while the sons become millionaire vice-presidents, young adults thrust into executive positions before they're

ready. The process of passing on family businesses to the next generation can bring tensions to a full boil.

The equitable division of the family business is usually the most
problematic decision. Although I generally recommend equally dividing other assets, it's often not a good idea to try to equally divide a
business among the children. Even though you may want to pass on
the business to the next generation, it's unlikely that your children will
have the desire or the ability to run the business exactly the way you
planned it.

If you can't figure out a way to pass it on successfully, think about
whether you should discontinue it, rather than inflicting it on another
generation.

Parents frequently make poor decisions when business and family
mix. A family hires a lazy son-in-law because otherwise he'll be unable
to support their daughter. A father hires his son for an executive position not because he's the most qualified candidate but because he can't
find a job elsewhere. Parents offer their daughter a job, not to give her
a great opportunity, but to keep her from taking their grandchildren
and moving to another state.

I counsel families struggling with these issues to think in terms of
the business members' happiness. Their decisions should foster the
children's healthy development and support the family economically. If
it doesn't do these things, the business should be sold before it destroys
the family, and vice versa.

Making It Work: A Few Family Business Guidelines

If you're passing on a family company, the following are a few
guidelines you'll want to keep in mind.

 Start early. Once you've made the decision to keep the business, it's
never too early to begin laying the groundwork for succession. If you
don't plan properly, a valuable business can end up being worth next
to nothing by the time it gets dragged through the messy estate settlement process. A well-planned succession takes between five and fifteen
years.

I usually recommend establishing an oversight committee com-
prised of family members and outside professionals such as lawyers

and family business consultants. The presence of these impartial outside experts can be invaluable in avoiding conflicts and hurt feelings along the way.

Even after you choose a successor, it takes years for them to gain the necessary training and experience, both outside and inside the company, to take on a top leadership position. The successor needs to learn to deal with both the headaches and responsibilities of various positions in the business and to work harmoniously with the employees, without whose support and confidence an orderly transition may be impossible.

In some cases even your best efforts don't pan out. The child, no matter how motivated or how much the parents want them to take over, may simply not be capable of doing the job. As heartbreaking as this scenario is, the parent must decide if he will risk the probable failure of both his child and the company. If not, the parents must select an outside successor, or sell the business. No matter what the scenario, all of this takes time, so the earlier you start the greater the chance for success.

Openly discuss each child's potential role. Have a family meeting, or a series of meetings, to discuss each child's interest in the business. Be realistic. Not every child will want the job, and those who do may not be qualified.

If your son, an artist, says he hopes to take the helm of your computer-consulting firm, insist that he must train in the computer and business management fields. Most kids who aspire to take over the family business must undergo an extensive grooming period that usually involves years of training and a hands-on apprenticeship. Ideally, the prospective successor spends several years "making it" on the outside before even coming into the family business.

Iron out the sticky issues up front. When it comes to divvying up a business, two's a crowd. If more than one child wants to take over, have them independently evaluated by a corporate psychologist who can offer an objective report on their strengths and developmental needs.

If your child is deemed less than competent for the job, you'll find yourself in the delicate position of having to explain the situation to the child who was not chosen for succession. First, be sure the corporate psychologist sits down with your child candidate and provides him or her with detailed results of the evaluation—especially the child's corresponding strengths and developmental needs. This is crucial to help the child understand why he and the job may not be the best fit.

Sometimes I have the parent sit in with me as I provide the child this feedback, to help them both talk through the situation. The parent or the child, based on this kind of objective feedback, may decide to pursue a remediation program to bring the kid up to par. If not, the company founder can say, "I know you've had your heart set on taking over the company, but we can see you're not the best person for the job right now. We'll have to develop you for some other opportunities in or out of the business, but I want to make sure it's something that's good for you and for our company."

If you have non-family candidates, run them through the same evaluation process to get the information that can aid your decision. Corporate or industrial psychologists are experts who, by virtue of their training and experience, can help you deal with these complex people-issues. Ask your accountant or attorney, or talk to the local Chamber of Commerce for a referral.

From these evaluation results, the succession committee can choose the successor and if necessary, mandate a development plan. If you should decide to leave the business to more than one child, which I usually discourage, be sure they can work well together in what are clearly defined roles and authorities.

Also, remember to figure out the compensation arrangements. Just because the kids aren't interested in the business doesn't mean they aren't looking to get some of the proceeds should you sell it. Make sure you're clear about who gets what.

Protect your income stream and retirement. Establish your assets and future retirement income independently of the business. If you don't, you won't be able to let go of control, because your income depends on the continuing performance of the business. This is a formula for disaster. You'll end up playing the role of the anxious founder hanging around and constantly second-guessing his successor.

Parents are right to be concerned. I've seen more than one set of elderly parents become financially destitute after their ne'er-do-well child ran a formerly prosperous business into the ground. Take the case of Joe, who owned and ran a large beer distributorship until he unexpectedly dropped dead of a heart attack. With no succession plan in place, his wife Vera, who had no experience running the company, took over. After a few frustrating weeks, she gave their young son Sal a job as president. Sal knew even less about running a regional distributorship. But the two struggled on.

Things went along fine for several months before the wheels started falling off. Key employees became disgruntled and began quitting, the economy soured, accounts started drying up, and profitability slumped. Vera panicked when she realized the business her husband had spent his life building—and that was her primary source of income—was going down the tubes. By the time she took over from Sal, the value of the business had nearly halved. She decided to sell anyway. Sad to say, Vera didn't get the best price. In fact, she got clobbered, leaving her to live out her life on a marginal income. This depressing story is repeated numerous times in this country every year.

One simple way to avoid this nightmare is to sell the business to the child and write the terms of sale in such a way to afford you an income, ensuring that you enjoy a financially comfortable old age. But be absolutely certain the child is competent to do the job of sustaining your business, and ultimately, your livelihood.

If you don't want to sell the business, you also have the option of leaving the business in trust for the children. This involves appointing an impartial outsider, such as a bank trust department, to oversee the operations of the business after your death. This sometimes becomes necessary when parents leave the business to one or more kids they don't think can handle it.

Leaving businesses to more than one child is often an invitation for disaster. Sure, some kids are good at sharing power, and some aren't. If children can be taught to work as equal partners, fine. But in a lot of cases, adding money to the quest for control of a substantial company is like throwing gas on a fire, fueling the mother of all family feuds.

Toss a few spouses into the mix and you're left with a rolling cauldron of emotions—jealousy, resentment, and anger—that can result in a nasty explosion.

Jerry, a client of mine, lived long enough to see his two sons rise in his insurance and financial services firm. He actually lived long enough to see them have knockdown, drag-out fights every week in their executive committee meetings. They just couldn't get along, but neither wanted to leave the company and strike out on their own. Yet neither were capable of taking over the firm and running it. As he considered succession, Jerry knew Phil and Jim wouldn't be able to run the business together once he wasn't around to pound his fist on the desk to put an end to their constant bickering.

As much as he hated doing it, Jerry employed the trust department of a bank to oversee the business for seven years after his death. In short, the bank took over Daddy's role and mediated as Phil and Jim continued to duke it out over every decision. I met with them on several occasions as meeting after meeting they wrangled, until finally over time, they were able to work out a way of working together. By year five of the seven they presented a united front to the bank trustees. By year seven, they ran the business as a team. Jerry's foresight and strong leadership had prevented the loss of the family business and ensured it's continued success, and therefore, the continued financial support of the family.

If all else fails and the succession plan seems unworkable, you can always cash out. But then the sale of the business raises other concerns. As difficult as transferring or selling the family business can be, there are also those nagging questions about what to do with other valuable assets.

Dollar Distributions: How Much Is Too Much?

The way people acquire money has a lot to do with what they do with it. Most wealthy people today acquired their money the old fashioned way: through a lifetime of working and putting it aside. Other than winning lottery tickets and big divorce settlements, the more common path to instant riches is inheriting a fortune or a successful family business. We've talked about the transfer of the family business. Now let's focus on the passing on the cash.

Nearly all parents worry that a fat inheritance will cause their children to become spoiled. Even thought I do believe there's a way to provide children some security without destroying their character, parents still need to be wary of dropping lottery-sized jackpots into their kids' laps.

I've already alluded to some of the dangers of inherited wealth including damaged self-esteem, ruined relationships, and shattered careers. Particularly when money comes early in life, wealth shelters the recipient from many of the difficult character building tasks of life. Abundance becomes a curse instead of blessing. As in Josh Adkins case, the son of overindulgent parents, this leaves them weaker and even less prepared for life's many challenges.

Let's revisit the Sloans and their decision about what to leave their grown sons. They knew they had blown it by giving the boys large cash gifts and hoped to find some way to correct for their mistake. They wanted to use the boy's inheritance as an incentive to do something useful with their lives. The options were limited. What could they do now to push their sons to do more?

As I sat in my office observing their puzzled faces, I decided to go for broke. "What law says you owe your kids an inheritance? Their money's running short. If you leave them nothing, they may be forced to carve out their own place in the world. Do you have the guts to leave your sons nothing and let them know it now?"

Henry and Sandy sat in stunned silence. I could quickly gauge from their reaction that they'd never before considered such a prospect. As so many affluent heads of households in this country, they had always felt obligated to pass on their assets to their children without realizing there were other alternatives. What I had said had struck a nerve.

I expected them to flatly reject my suggestion. I was surprised when Henry finally asked, "How would we go about that?"

"Leave your kids some money," I suggested, "but just enough to allow them to have a bare-bones existence. It should be enough for them to get by but not so much that they can avoid having to get a job. Then leave the rest to your favorite charity."

The more they thought about the idea, the more they liked it. With this plan the boys would be forced to get a life. In the months that followed the Sloans worked with their attorney to piece together a family foundation that would distribute their substantial wealth to their selected charities after they died.

Will the Sloans "reality therapy" work? Their children probably won't feel the full sting of inheriting nothing until after their deaths. But as far as each child knows, all they're going to get is $200,000 each, distributed through a trust only for educational and dire health needs. Beyond that, they are completely on their own. Henry and Sandy still hope this message will push their kids to do something with their lives while they're still young.

Many parents struggle with the same tough question: how much can we leave our kids without ruining them?

Even as parents decide the *when* of giving, they're still haunted by the decision of *how much*. Many affluent parents, whether they've come into money suddenly or earned and saved it over a lifetime, agonize over this question. How can we enrich our children's lives but not ruin them by giving too much?

Parents run the gamut. Billionaire investor Warren Buffet in a Fortune article said he was leaving his children very little, "a few hundred thousand dollars." He's decided to leave most of his money to charity because giving children, "a lifetime supply of food stamps just because they came out of the right womb" would be "harmful" to them.

Other super-wealthy parents, such as Jackson Stephens, chairman of the huge investment bank Jackson Stephens, Inc., takes a totally different position. He said, "I'd rather give my money to my kids than do anything else with it. If my heirs want to clip coupons, that'll be their business. I can't control their future, and I'm not going to worry a whole bunch."

I invariably talk over these issues with my clients, help them gauge their own feelings, and try to guide them to a decision that makes them feel comfortable. They all want to leave their kids enough money to lead fuller lives but not so much that they don't have to get up to go to work in the morning. Unfortunately, there is no single number that can ensure your child's welfare without wrecking his self-esteem.

You may have a daughter who is an exceptionally talented artist, makes $20,000 a year, and by most standards is an economic failure. Another family may have a son who's proving to be a hard-charger on his own, so no matter how much you leave him it won't make much of a difference in the way he runs his life. Still another son may be struggling to find himself. He may need help, but not so much help that he gives up the struggle.

We talked about the way inherited wealth, granted without discipline and unearned except by birthright, leaves a person crippled emotionally and psychologically. Michael Crichton expressed this idea in the fictional monologue of Ian Malcolm, the scientist in *Jurassic Park*; "I will tell you what I am talking about," he said. "Most kinds of power require a substantial sacrifice by whoever wants the power. There is an apprenticeship, a discipline lasting years. Whatever kind of power you want. President of the company. Black belt in karate. Spiritual guru. Whatever it is you seek, you have to put in the time, the practice, the effort. You must put in a lot to get it. It has to be very important to you. And once you have attained it, it is your power. It can't be given away: it resides in you. It is literally the result of your discipline. Now, what is interesting about this process is that, by the time someone has acquired the ability to kill with their bare hands, he has also matured to the point where he won't use it unwisely. So that kind of power has built-in control. The discipline of getting the power changes you so that you won't abuse it. But scientific power is like inherited wealth: attained without discipline."

Heirs all too often develop a distorted sense of themselves and others, not having experienced the effort, cultivated the relationships, or attained the character and leadership associated with achieving their fortune firsthand.

The key factor in the "how much" decision is based on true need and character. The greater the true need, as with a handicapped child, or the stronger the child's character, as with the child who has established herself independently, the larger the gift. The smaller the true need and weaker the character, the greater chance any gift will cause problems.

I believe that in most cases less is better. If you're focused on helping your kids lead happy, fulfilling lives, very little of that has to do with their having huge sums of money. As long as their, and even their children's most basic needs are met – food, shelter, medical, love and limits – whether they're happy or fulfilled is really up to them. It's not something you or anybody can bequeath in a will or by writing a fat check. Happiness is an inside job.

But you still want a number. Even though every parent faces a somewhat different challenge, I do know one rule of thumb that works no matter what the particular situation. Remember the first Law of Financial Parenting. "Too much" is any amount that robs them of their self-esteem or undermines their ambition. Think very carefully how this rule applies in your own kids' lives and if you're going to err, err by giving less instead of more. It's a lot easier to go back later and add than it is to subtract.

Now let's look at some of the last, yet most important financial decisions you will make in your lifetime.

Chapter Thirteen:

Securing Your Legacy:
The Psychology of Formulating Wills,
Estates and Trusts

Inherited wealth…is as certain a death
to ambition as cocaine is to morality.
—Commodore Vanderbilt's Grandson

"We've put it off long enough. Nancy and I have to sit down and make some tough decisions about what to do with our estate," moaned Chuck Drysdale, a personal injury attorney who had amassed quite a fortune over the course of his long career. "Being a lawyer, you'd think I would have taken care of this years ago. It's facing the gut-wrenching decisions about the kids that makes this so difficult."

Many affluent parents identify with Chuck and Nancy's hesitation. Prosperous parents typically approach estate planning with a mixture of fear, dread and confusion. Not only can they can relate to the hard work and difficult emotional decisions stirred up in the process, they've also heard the horror stories of families destroyed by their wealth. Arthur Vanderbilt tells one such story in *Fortune's Children,* where he recounts the decadence and decline one of the nation's most conspicuous millionaire families.

You don't have to be a Vanderbilt or a Rockefeller to be anxious about handling the delicate issues of leaving money to your kids. These are some of the most challenging decisions parents will make in their lives. I would rank these decisions as just as important as getting married, having children or choosing a career. Let me offer a word of advice before you get started: get some good advice!

Questions of the Heart: Talking With Your Financial Advisors

Many affluent parents make the mistake of trying to handle all of the aspects of wealth transfer on their own. Refusing to consult professionals, sooner or later, they make foolish mistakes that prove costly, both financially and psychologically, resulting in bitter family legacies. Financial professionals can help you to avoid this heartbreak. With their assistance, you will be able to navigate around the traps that so often hurt those you've spent your life trying to help.

I've personally witnessed, a long parade of horrible, and often preventable, estate planning blunders. I've seen fortunes earned over lifetimes squandered in a few short years: the daughter who magnanimously bestowed her entire inheritance to a cult, the son who overdosed on the cocaine purchased out of his sudden windfall, the sibling who walked away with the money he received to care for his disabled brother. I've also observed nasty legal battles between the "good" kids and their "good for nothing" disinherited sibling. The bigger the fortune involved, the nastier the conflicts.

Whether you're dealing with matters of the head or the heart, begin by seeking the advice of trusted professionals. Your first team of advisors should involve a tax or probate attorney and in most cases your accountant or financial planner. Be sure your attorney and accountant specialize in estate planning, or at least work in a firm that employs such a specialist. You'll likely need to consult with your broker, insurance agent, banker, and an appraiser as well. The size of the team depends largely on the size and complexity of your assets.

Start building your estate planning team by meeting with a financial professional you already know and trust, then ask them to guide you in picking other team members. Set meetings to interview any prospective professional candidates to make sure you're comfortable with their style and competence. Don't be shy. These are some of the most important decisions you'll make in your lifetime. Don't hesitate to ask questions about their experience with issues that concern you, whether they're members of professional associations like the Council on Estate Planners, and how many estate plans they've done over their careers. If the professional won't or can't answer your questions, keep looking.

As a rule of thumb, families with more complex situations – business owners and people with substantial assets – should be prepared to work with a formidable team of professionals. Whatever the eventual make-up of your team, it is absolutely essential that your advisors communicate and coordinate with each other on your various plan components.

Your team of advisors will be particularly helpful in dealing with many of the legal and financial aspects of estate planning. But they're not likely to be able to help much with the more emotional facets of estate planning, the decisions of the heart. These aspects are every bit as important as the income statements and the legal forms. For guidance on these issues, seek the advice of a trusted priest, minister, family counselor, close friend or family member. These individuals can help you to better understand your own feelings, values, and needs throughout the estate planning process. They can also help in sorting out the messy family dynamics, like sibling rivalries or divided loyalties, that are often exacerbated when moneys involved. Try to locate a professional counselor who's also experienced and trained in the issues of family wealth counseling.

Conversely, when it's hardcore financial advice you need, trust your team to give you the straight scoop. Friends and relatives are there for emotional support, not expert advice. That favorite uncle who knows you so well is best qualified to help you understand some of the personal needs and beliefs embedded in major life decisions. But beware the friend or cousin dispensing financial advice. If you do listen, take what they offer with at least a few grains of salt.

The true bottom line for parents is to strike a balance between professional and personal advice when deciding what to do with your estate. Finding the right answers takes time and careful deliberation.

Sometimes all the technical and friendly advice in the world isn't enough. If, after digesting the advice of your estate planning "dream team," you still find yourself uncertain about what to do, call for a second opinion.

Let's look at the ways some parents have negotiated this passage.

Golden Giving: Smart Moves in the Transfer of Wealth

Warren and Susan Buffet and Bill and Melinda Gates have one thing in common. No, it's not the fact that they are both multi-billionaires.

They've both announced that they are leaving their substantial estates largely to charity.

Warren Buffet didn't disinherit his children because he disapproved of their career choices or their character. In fact at the time he made this announcement, his daughter was an administrative assistant to the editor of *US News and World Report* and his son a successful farmer. His desire was to "force them to carve out their own place in the world." He was determined to leave them "enough money so they could do anything, but not so much that they could do nothing."

The Buffets' and the Gates' decisions reflect a broader trend: affluent parents are becoming seriously concerned about the effects of passing on large estates to their offspring. They recognize that flooding their children with oceans of unearned income can drown their psyches.

Andrew Carnegie, the wealthy steel magnate, wrote, "I would as soon leave my son a curse as the almighty dollar." Mr. Carnegie was not alone in his sentiment. This is an idea that has gained increasing momentum over the last several years. Now, more then ever, rich parents are more carefully considering the potential negative fall-out of large gifts, and are becoming more creative in these transfers of wealth.

I interviewed a number of estate attorneys, accountants, and financial planners: specialists who work daily with affluent families, helping them figure out how to best transfer wealth from one generation to the next. Many of these financial professionals told their own sad stories about clients whose wealth had become more of a burden than a blessing. They also shared with me the keys to avoiding this tragedy.

160

Their number one piece of advice: make sure you *have* a will. Although most owners of substantial estates make a formal estate plan, 60% of all estates in America transfer without a will or trust. If you fail to make a will before you die, the courts refer to you as having "died intestate," and then step in to make one for you. They will decide how to disburse your property, pick a guardian for your children and select an administrator. Without a formal will, you will lose the chance to have your personal wishes legally protected.

Act now. Look at the lessons you can teach your kids. It's a great opportunity to practice some of what you've learned about financial parenting.

Getting the Estate Planning Ball Rolling

If you haven't yet developed your inheritance plan—and the majority of you probably haven't—there are a few things you must do, preferably in consultation with experts in the field. To begin, write a basic statement of your wishes: who will inherit, what they will receive, when the inheritance will occur, and any special conditions that apply. If you have kids, name an executor who will carry out your instructions. Many people automatically leave everything to their spouse, and ultimately to their kids. But what if your present mate isn't your first, or you have two sets of children? The dynamics of giving become particularly tricky in blended families. Don't trust the courts to dispose of your estate—you know your family better than any judge could.

Besides the directives on distributions of assets, some parents are drafting what are called ethical wills. Ethical wills focus on passing on your most cherished values, with the hope that these gifts of the heart, mind and spirit will be preserved and cherished. Author Barry Baines offers guidance in this process in his book, *Ethical Wills: Putting Your Values on Paper*.

If your children are not yet 18, you also need to specify a guardian to care for your minor dependents. Your guardian, or trustee, may be a trusted sibling, friend or a professional.

Name a back-up person for both the job of executor and the job of trustee, and make sure they all know where your will is kept. Most people maintain the original in a safe deposit box with a copy in their attorney's office. Make sure the beneficiaries on your brokerage and retirement accounts and insurance policies conform to your will.

You should also draft what's called a standby guardianship proxy for your children's guardian to be kept right next to your will. This document authorizes the guardian to make decisions about your child's health and finances until the court certifies guardianship. The designated trustee, if different than your guardian, should have a standby power of attorney. Additionally all parents, no matter what their age or their kids' ages, should have a fully executed health care proxy as well as a living will or medical directive. These documents instruct the health-care provider whether to take certain steps to pro-long your life.

Do your kids a favor. If you lack any of this basic paperwork, put it together now. You don't want to wait until you're incapacitated and can't communicate, or even worse, dead. I've seen firsthand how this kind of procrastination has caused devastating problems for the sur-viving family members. Look at this as another great opportunity, per-haps your last, to teach your kids some valuable financial and life lessons.

When you have it all together, make sure your attorney has a copy of your will, durable power of attorney, medical directives, funeral and burial instructions and trust documents. Your safe deposit box or home safe should contain deeds and titles, birth certificates, military discharge papers, marriage licenses, home inventory, divorce decrees, stock certificates, Social Security cards, pension plans, insurance poli-cies, wills, medical directives, a list of brokerage and bank accounts, certificates of deposit, seven years of tax returns, credit card accounts, and a list of any other legal documents you've left with your attorney.

If this all sounds like a lot of work, it is. But do it anyway.

Protecting Your Money and Your Kids

While increasing numbers of parents are considering charitable giving, others still wish to leave their assets to their kids, but they want to be sure these gifts bring blessings instead of curses. As the bulk of this book illustrates, their concern over the impact of wealth is well founded.

Naturally, parents consult with advisors every day, searching for strategies that will affect their children and grandchildren in positive ways. What parent hasn't, at some time or another, wanted to influence the behavior of their children? We've talked about using allowances and other consequences to teach children responsible behavior from age three. Even when we get to estate planning, parenting's final frontier, the same principles still apply. As our children get older, the tools we use to influence them just become a bit more sophisticated.

Where once we encouraged responsible behavior through our children's allowances, we will now do the same thing by establishing their trusts, which can function like allowances for big kids. Trusts are simply legal documents that spell out the conditions by which assets will be distributed. They also protect the trustee who is carrying out the donor's wishes from frivolous liability. Trusts are for anyone with young children, older "problem children" (adult Silver Spooners, for example) or aged parents for whom you wish to provide. Trusts can also keep Uncle Sam's tax bite to a minimum.

Let me mention a few cautions about using trusts. First, don't make the mistake of thinking trusts are only for the super-rich. Trusts are for anyone with after-death assets of more than a few thousand dollars. Don't forget that life insurance proceeds alone can swell a modest nest egg into a sizeable chunk of cash. Second, be realistic. No legal document, no matter how cleverly drafted, can make up for years of lousy child rearing. At best, it may keep the damage from going forward. As you work with your attorney preparing these types of documents, be crystal clear about what you want to accomplish, but don't expect miracles from a mere piece of paper.

Your trust can help you promote certain behaviors, although it is by no means a guarantee. If your intention is to encourage entrepreneurship, state this clearly. If you want your children to complete their college degree as a condition of inheritance, say so.

It's better to figure out these objectives before you start the meter with your lawyer. Also, make sure that the trustee you choose to manage the trust, be it a family member, friend, or professional, is strong, firm, fair and up to the job. It's also a good idea to name a back-up trustee in the event your first pick becomes unable, or unwilling, to serve.

Trust Funds for the Good, the Bad and the Ugly

What behaviors do most parents want to address in their children's trusts?

The Good: At the top of the list for most of the parents I've dealt with is the pursuit of an education. Most of these parents set up trusts to reimburse the child for all educational expenses, from private secondary school straight through to their post-graduate or professional degrees. Few would argue against the value of a good education.

Many parents seek to encourage a positive work ethic by their gifts. This goal is often attempted by the use of incentive trusts, which reward hard work and accomplishment—or in other words, prompt late-bloomers to "get a life." Incentive trusts reward beneficiaries when they accomplish certain specific objectively measurable criteria. For example, children may receive a specified amount of money when they graduate from college, join the family business, earn a graduate degree, overcome a drug or alcohol problem or give something back to the community through charitable volunteer work.

Many parents also wish to encourage altruism. I've seen this more in established wealth, where the heads of the family want to communicate the value of service to their offspring. In these cases the donors provide special supplements for those children who become nurses, teachers, college professors, artists, social workers and the like.

A common kin to altruism is philanthropy. Many well-off parents with philanthropic tendencies feel the "noblesse oblige," the responsibility of the wealthy to create good. They want to see these obligations carried on into the next generations. They seek to accomplish this goal by involving their children early and consistently in philanthropic activities such as family foundations, donor advised funds, charitable trusts and the like.

These parents gently guide the younger generation's experience in their work as trustees, general partners or asset managers. In this way, kids learn the value of stewardship while being exposed to the practical process of building and preserving assets for future generations. Some families make this a tradition, and pass it down from one generation to the next.

The Bad: On the other side of the coin, estate planning sometimes forces parents to take a stand against certain problematic behaviors in their adult kids. Interestingly, one of the biggest problems affluent parents try to discourage is reckless consumption. This is ironic, since many of these same parents are themselves prodigious consumers, and have often promoted that very behavior in their children. Sometimes these anti-squander plans will hold up an immature child's inheritance until the risk of dissipation is gone—or at least minimized. If the situation justifies delay until your children are in their forties, fifties or sixties, then so be it. By delaying allocation until then, you have protected the family money *from* your child and *for* your child.

Many parents also want to discourage sloth and laziness. Typically, their kids don't really intend to join the work-a-day world and would rather subsist on whatever they can wheedle out of their parents, grandparents, and trustees. These loafers are usually good candidates for incentive trusts.

One father I counseled set up an incentive trust to support his son's working. In this "earn a dollar, get a dollar" arrangement the trustee was authorized to pay the exact amount annually equal to the sons "wages, tips, salaries as indicated on line seven of his U.S. tax return for the previous year." Another set of parents established a trust that distributed the sum of $10,000 on the 15th of each month only if their son was gainfully employed during the whole of the preceding month. Gainful employment was verified when the child presented a valid pay stub that indicated he had been paid for at least 80 hours the prior month. I've seen many variations on this same theme.

The Ugly: Just as the wild spender and chronic loafer present challenges to parents, so also does the child or grandchild with obvious self-destructive behavior. This most often takes the form of alcohol or drug abuse, criminal behavior, or frank mental illness. In these situations the planning and drafting of economic incentives is focused primarily on discouraging destructive behavior while supporting more positive alternative choices. Parents want to avoid, at all costs, "enabling" their child's destruction. Incentive trusts were designed for just this type of dilemma.

I often advise parents to align their influence with their deepest concerns. In these scenarios the donor parent needs to replace handouts, often motivated by guilt, pity or fear, with well-thought-out standards for distributions from the trust. The goal is to remove subjective factors and feelings that work against the best interest of the child. Similarly, the parent, trustee and donor need to eliminate sympathy and manipulation as a basis for discretionary distributions.

Incentive trusts aren't a panacea for such problems, but they have their advantages. They can eliminate the emotional blackmail beneficiaries often inflict upon their parents and trustees. By introducing objectivity, the incentive trust creates a clear contract and restores the adult child's dignity. Now they can decide for themselves, of their own free will, whether they want to go along with their parent's wishes or not.

Again I think it's important for parents to be reasonable in their goals. I discourage parents from using incentive trusts to attempt to control a child's choice of spouse, faith, occupation or school. Wisdom dictates that we not try to coerce compliance when compliance is unlikely.

Incentive trusts come with a few inherent disadvantages. By design, they aren't as flexible as discretionary trusts. Additionally, incentive trusts often require some measurement on the part of the trustee. Whether it's checking pay stubs, drug tests, or transcripts, somebody has to monitor behavior and make decisions about consequences.

Naturally, some kids resent having to report in. They may decide they'd rather forgo the economic benefits than subject themselves to a monthly urinalysis. That's their prerogative. But what if they try to cheat? Your trustee could be in for endless headaches, trying to determine whether the lab tests were altered, or whether the beneficiary really worked the hours. It's not possible to plan for every contingency.

In my consultation with families I've seen incentive trusts work best in truly desperate situations—usually as a last resort. If a parent is preparing to disinherit a child for his dysfunctional behavior, an incentive trust gives the child one last opportunity to change in order to avoid disinheritance.

Discretionary trusts are usually preferable to incentive trusts because they afford trustees greater flexibility in their decisions.

However, you do need to spell out clear guidelines as to the exercise of discretion. As a rule of thumb, the healthier the family, the better chance they can afford the greater flexibility of a discretionary trust. In these more flexible arrangements, some parents let their children have access to their money for specific purposes such as education, buying a house, or to supplement healthcare costs. Other parents dole out inheritances in installments, say one-third at age 25, another third at 30, and the remainder at 35.

Incentive and discretionary trusts are just a few examples of the dozens of wealth transfer options open to you. There are a myriad of tricky family situations—disabled children, multiple marriages, surviving spouses, taxes and so forth—that are well beyond the scope of this book. Fortunately there are some excellent resources available. Do some research, ask what your friends are doing, talk to an attorney, and then consider which legal vehicle best suits your particular family circumstances.

Once you've made your decision and put it all down on paper, you're ready for the next big hurdle: what to tell the kids.

Avoiding Inheritance Battles: Clearly Communicating What's What

As a parent, you know how important it is to talk to your children about sex, drugs, alcohol and other uncomfortable topics. But as we age, we seem to become more reluctant to talk about such subjects as money and the distribution of our belongings. As uncomfortable as it may be, these discussions are some of the most important talks we'll ever have with our children.

We've talked about the importance of openly discussing finances with children from an early age. Kids feel more secure when their parents encourage questions about money, and answer them frankly. Unfortunately, many parents keep their children in the dark about their inheritances. Some do it to control their behavior; more parents withhold this information trying to protect them from what they believe is a burdensome responsibility. Overly protective, they subscribe to the "what they don't know won't hurt them" school of parenting.

The truth is, what they don't know *can* hurt them.

Kids need to know what they can expect, even if it's bad news. If you don't discuss the stipulations of the wills or trusts before your death, your inheritors will be left with the difficult task of interpreting your meaning and intent on their own. This will only add confusion to the grief and loss they're already experiencing. You can only save them this pain by openly discussing your estate plans with your heirs. If you're favoring one beneficiary over another, it's important that they know why. With time and luck, they will understand and accept your decisions. In some instances, these confrontations trigger healthy change. Try to resolve any conflicts and differences, and make peace before it's too late.

I believe a parent's job, and often their last great gift, as tough as it may be, is to make decisions about the distribution of their assets and communicate those decisions to their loved ones.

Tips on Holding The Family Money Meeting

Take the bull by the horns. Arrange a meeting with your family to talk about your estate. Be sure to have a complete understanding of your net worth. If you haven't totaled up everything you own, the chore is probably overdue. Once you fully understand your estate, sit down with your kids and cover all of the relevant financial information at one time. If you expect things to be particularly difficult or unpleasant, think about bringing in an objective third party to serve as a mediator. You could invite your attorney or financial professional, or if you're fearful of your child's reaction, you may wish to bring in a family psychologist.

Sometimes an experienced family wealth counselor can help you present this type of delicate information, and can head off problems before they develop. Even in extremely sticky situations, a counselor can minimize the squabbles that often arise. The key is to anticipate the conflict. Get this help *before* you have the actual discussion of your estate. Once you've announced your estate, the damage is done. It then becomes impossible to get the proverbial horse back into the barn.

Before you hold your meeting, decide precisely what it is you wish to accomplish. Be sure you and your spouse are on the same page. If you disagree on key points, iron this out between yourselves before you involve the children or make any public statements. Create a list of the people who should be there. Choose what you wish to say, and think of how best to say it. You may even want to rehearse your talk beforehand. Anticipate problems. Create a fallback plan. Do whatever you need to do to prepare yourself emotionally for what could happen. Be prepared for the worst, but hope for the best.

Go over as much detail as you think is necessary. We've all heard tales of heirs raiding the parent's home after the funeral. It's often the smallest items, particularly if they hold strong sentimental value, that cause the longest-lasting emotional reaction and potential damage.

When it comes to dividing up the antiques, silver, jewelry, and photos, people never forget it if they didn't get what they thought they had coming to them. If you've promised a certain item to a certain child, keep your promise.

Most parents prefer to divide their assets equally among their kids for a number of reasons. They don't want to show favoritism; they love them equally; or they don't want there to be bad blood among the kids once they're gone. The Gediman study noted that, "you can treat your children unequally while you're alive, but after you die it becomes 'official,' a kind of immortal black mark."

"I don't want to be cussed from my grave," one client told me.

If you do decide to make unequal distributions, such as with a handicapped child, think it through and discuss it with your advisors.

Clarify all of these decisions and document them in your will or living trust. If you want to keep this information about your possessions private, put it in a side letter. Some parents tag or photograph possessions to keep track of them. However you go about this process, just be sure you've talked openly about the division of property.

Head off the obvious problems wherever possible. If you can visualize your kids wrestling over the Jaguar keys in the driveway of the funeral home, sell it and decide how to split the proceeds.

If you care about maintaining family harmony, leave your money and property to your kids equally, regardless of their economic circumstances. To fail to do so can leave deep emotional wounds that never heal. I've heard siblings complain bitterly about their favored sister getting an extra piece of jewelry twenty years after their mother's death. This kind of perceived "parental favoritism" can lead to family breakups, lawsuits, and in some cases, violence. This becomes particularly dicey when there are children from a second marriage involved.

This equal economic treatment should have begun well before your kids received their inheritance. It should apply to all the gifts you give to your kids over their lifetime. If you paid for one son's college, or gave him a down payment for a first home, then do something equivalent for the other kids. If you leave the family business to your oldest, work out something comparable for the siblings.

Of course, use common sense. You don't have to leave your unemployed alcoholic a lump of cash just because you gave his physician sister a medical school education. *Don't* reward failure and punish success. Tailor your gifts carefully, in the best interest of each child.

Don't get stuck trying to make sure everyone's perfectly happy. Lay it out for them from the beginning: "It may not be what each of you thinks is fair, but it's the way I feel most comfortable dealing with the situation." If they don't like it, too bad. Tell your kids, "We love you and respect the choices you're making in your life, but it's our money, we made it, and this is what we've decided to do with it. At some point you will receive something from us but it won't be enough to live on easy street so you'll have to continue to work hard and build your own fortune."

Whatever you have to tell them, I'd advise parents to serve it up straight. Be frank with your kids about what they stand to inherit. Gather your children and tell them, "The fact that we have $3 million doesn't mean that you can quit your jobs tomorrow. There will be taxes, we have some charities we're giving to, and the rest will be split and placed in trusts to provide for certain needs. So don't sit around and wait for the big check. Go on with your lives."

If parents don't have that kind of dialogue, some kids hang out waiting for the big jackpot. It's a parental duty to deal directly with these issues. I think kids are ready for these talks at the youngest in their mid-teens—and at the latest, when they hit college age.

This kind of open, direct communication becomes especially important when one parent becomes ill, incapacitated, or may need to change their circumstances, such as when one parent is dying or requires placement in a long-term care facility. In such unfortunate circumstances, it's nearly impossible to pull this off without considerable hardship for all involved.

As I've said, don't wait until then. Do it now.

Spending Down: The Advantages of Dying Broke

"I want to die with a quarter in my pocket," quipped Jake, a well-heeled businessman who was sitting on a hard-earned fortune. People joke about leaving behind nothing but a check for the undertaker—and the check, of course, bounces. As Mark Levine and Stephen Pollan discuss in their thought-provoking book *Die Broke*, there's something to be said for cutting it close. After all, when was the last time you saw luggage racks on a hearse?

Let's face it. We're all living on this earth on borrowed time and while we're here, not just time, but *everything we have is borrowed.* Whether we've borrowed way more than our fair share, or way less, we end up having to give it back when we go. In this section we're going to offer two ways to give it back while you're still around.

The "die broke" approach gives you one huge advantage: you don't have to worry about the way your money might affect your kids after you're gone! No fusses over fancy, complicated trusts, no concerns about interfamily squabbling, and no worry about your money ruining your progeny's motivation. You don't have to sweat over whether you might be showing favoritism to one kid or another, you don't have to work out distinctions between "natural" children and stepchildren, and you'll have no need to keep a leash on your kid's predatory spouse. This form of estate planning is easy on the blood pressure!

But don't expect to hear this philosophy coming from the mouths of traditional financial gurus. In fact, this advice flies in the face of everything a sensible planner says to do! Conventional wisdom urges you to protect, nurture, and grow your estate. But even though this novel approach raises the hairs on the back of the necks of most financial planners, it does have some merit. Spend your money wisely now, or give it all away. Leave this world with what you came in with - nothing. How's that for a simple, clean exit strategy?

The idea behind spending it all before you die is not to live foolishly, but to rethink the reasons why you're holding onto what you have for some distant tomorrow that may never come. Levine and Pollan tell us to use our money *today* to take care of our loved ones and ourselves. Live well and enjoy your assets while you're still alive. Readily available financial tools can insure that you won't outlive your money and will still guarantee that you'll leave nothing behind. For some, this is the way to go.

We've all seen the bumper sticker, "We're spending our children's inheritance." Even if you plan to rid yourself of the burden of distributing your assets to your family, there are different ways of sharing wealth while you're alive.

Rather than waiting to leave your kids money after you die, you can choose to enrich their lives while you're around to enjoy it. I've seen wealthy parents buying vacation homes to enjoy with the extended family, taking family members on overseas vacations they couldn't otherwise take, or contributing to the down payment on their first home. I've known a number of affluent parents who've regularly gifted their kids the allowable $10,000 per year allotment with the stipulation that the money be invested for the future. Some have bypassed their kids and directly gifted the grandchildren as a way of endowing their education.

I think it's a great idea to help seed a grandchild's retirement plan and work with them as they watch it grow. One inexpensive and attractive way to set up a savings plan for your kid's or grandkid's long term future is through a unique mutual fund called the Twentieth Century Giftrust. The beauty of this fund is that it lets donors exercise some control over the gifts so that the investments enjoy the benefits of long-term compounding.

It's really pretty simple: you make a gift, the minimum is $250, to a trust account and name a beneficiary. Next you set the date at least ten years in the future when the person gets the money. You can pick the maturity date to come due when the beneficiary graduates college, buys their first home or is likely to retire. With compounding at a rate of 10%, that original seed would grow to $76,000 when they celebrate their 60th birthday.

By giving up the goal of accumulating a huge estate, you can also enjoy your own life more. Stop scrimping and saving for some distant future and spend the summers learning French cooking in Provence, buy a winter home for skiing in the Rockies, or just simply splurge on that Far East jaunt you've talked about for years. Free from the burden of having to preserve and distribute an estate, you're free to do whatever you want with the time you have left.

Positive Philanthropy: Giving It All Away

Philanthropy often serves as an attractive alternative for people who don't wish to leave substantial assets to their family, or who don't have family that could be beneficiaries. Parents choose this alternative for several reasons. Like the Buffets and the Gates, they may wish to protect their offspring from the potential ravages of riches. Others have become alienated from their kids and grandkids. Instead of leaving it to their families, they give it to charity out of spite. Still others create charitable foundations to refurbish a tarnished family name or to avoid taxes.

Of course, people also donate their estates to charity out of genuine altruism. Many individuals wish to "give back" to a college, a church, a hospital or a cause. Their altruism may also be part of larger plan to teach their kids and grandkids the importance of frugality, service and stewardship. Their giving, through charitable trusts and private foundations, benefits both their families and the larger community.

Some parents ask if they have enough money to start a family foundation. If you have at least $500,000, then you've got enough. Private foundations, which number in the thousands in this country, are particularly good vehicles to teach kids service and stewardship. Given that these foundations are private entities, parents or grandparents can select family members as directors and trustees. These children then have the privilege and responsibility of determining the charitable beneficiaries of the family funds.

To the extent that the parents wish, they can decide the focus of the foundation as well. For example, if the donor wishes to help their kids learn to appreciate the arts, they may create a structure that limits the charitable giving to arts organizations.

Whatever their focus, foundations give children the opportunity to learn more about the wider world of needs arrayed in the universe of charitable organizations. They're exposed to the principles of asset management and distribution. If the fund managers take their job seriously, it's hard for them not to develop some measure of altruism, energy for good works, and empathy for those less advantaged. These are all essential building blocks in the grooming of stewardship. Most children enjoy the activities necessary to run a private foundation. It's gratifying to give money to worthy causes. It also provides the giver with a certain stature in the community. For all these reasons, private foundations are a great idea to consider.

For parents who want many of the benefits of foundations without the administrative headaches, donor-advised funds have become popular substitutes for private foundations. Charles Schwab and a number of other financial management firms offer charitable gift accounts that greatly simplify the process of charitable giving and allow the children to be involved as donor-advisors. If neither of these options appeal to you but you still want to give your money away, you can always gift charitable contributions directly or through "independent" foundations.

Of course, not everyone's motivation is as pure as the driven snow. A less altruistic, though no less legitimate, reason for charitable giving is a desire for recognition and prestige. Some people have real concerns about the way they're regarded after their death. They want a lasting monument to their place on this earth, a testament to their greatness. Sometimes charitable giving is simply a smokescreen for good tax planning—not that there's anything wrong with saving taxes! It's not a bad deal, when you can give to your favorite charity and reap tax advantages at the same time! In a charitable remainder trust, for example, you're able to give your property in trust to a charity while still receiving income from the trust for your remaining years. After you die, the charity takes control of your assets.

Whatever your final decision, whether you establish a trust or a foundation, or whether you throw your money out of the window, beware the consequences! Take your time, consult with trusted professionals, think it through carefully, and consider all your options.

Remember that you only have one legacy to leave.

Loving Legacies: The True Measure of Success

"Margie and I did what we could to give our kids every advantage growing up," Jake said proudly as he reflected on his long and prosperous life, "I don't mean financially, in fact, some of our greatest gifts were holding back money and privileges. We let the children struggle; we let them see that they could make it themselves. That's been our largest contribution, to have raised two responsible boys who can take care of themselves and their families. I've always believed good parenting is getting your kids to the point where they can stand on their own."

We all hope to end up like Jake one day. We want to be able to look back over our lives and know we did our best. All our efforts pay off when our kids turn out happy, independent and wise. This is the true legacy we all want to leave.

Let's be honest. Whether you decide to leave everything to your children, fund a charity, or donate a building to your Alma matter, you're probably motivated in large part by your desire to be remembered. It's nothing to be embarrassed about. The desire to leave an immortalizing legacy is a powerful, normal human urge.

Yet as we've discussed, our desire to be proactive, to decide our conscious legacy, is often short-circuited by our reluctance to face our own mortality. We assume we're not going to die today, so we put off planning until tomorrow; or the next day, or the next week, or month, or year. Too many people run out of tomorrows before they run out of excuses, and these important decisions never get made.

Sure, you're busy with your career and your family, and rather than dealing with this sensitive issue, you avoid it. That's why over 60% of Americans die without a will. Don't let yourself wind up in that statistic! Take advantage of this golden opportunity to teach your children a final lesson—about life, about money, about yourself.

We start this process by accepting that our time on this earth is limited. Beginning with this fact, as we reflect on our lives, we begin to ask some of life's most difficult, yet meaningful questions. What have I done with my life? What am I leaving behind? How will my kids remember me?

I'm concerned about the way today's kids will fare. I worry that they're missing out on vital lessons that in generations past would have come from deeply involved parents, teachers and communities. Unless we give these children more of ourselves and less of our money, I'm afraid they won't be able to handle the challenges they will face. I worry that these children will lack the essential character they'll need to cope with life's ups and downs. Will they have the strength and determination to respond to the adversity and hardship they must inevitably face?

The final outcome of this generation largely depends on us. If we parents will find the time in our busy schedules to raise our children to be caring, responsible, charitable, and honest with themselves and others, instill in them a measured appreciation for the privileged world to which they've been born, give them the psychological tools to cope with stress and transcend adversity –in short, to help them develop inner strength and character – then there is hope.

Let's do our kids this favor. Let's leave them the kind of legacy that no amount of money can buy.

To keep our kids healthy, wealthy, and wise, we parents must live by the Laws of Financial Parenting. Keep these principles in your mind and heart as you interact with your children every day:

Safeguard the development of their ambition: Satisfy your child's true physical needs; question ruthlessly their myriad of wants. Once we've met our children's basic needs, providing financial support beyond that point is fraught with danger. Let them hunger for things— and help them develop the skills to satisfy their own hunger.

Foster their resilience and self-control: Your children need you to set limits on their behavior. They need you to be the parent. By all means, be on good terms with your children, but don't abdicate your parental authority. They need your leadership in order to learn how to lead themselves.

Help them become part of the human race: Don't let them equate their self-worth with their net worth. Give them what really counts: your love, your guidance, your time. There is nothing you can purchase that will make up for your absence in their lives. Be there. Be available.

Take an active interest in your children's lives. Find out what's going on in their hearts and minds. It's easier to find the time to do this when you recognize that *you have nothing to do that is more important than parenting your children.*

Give them the tools, and the desire, to manage money: Help them learn to value money properly. Take the time to teach them the skills and knowledge they need to keep their financial house in order, and instill in them the reason for doing so.

Model the values you want to see in them: As they say in Alcoholic Anonymous circles, if you're going to talk the talk, you've got to walk the walk. Take a hard look at yourself from time to time, to make certain that you're setting the example you want your kids to follow. If you want your child to be considerate of others, don't break in the line at the movie theatre. If you want your child to be compassionate, be kind to the handicapped neighbor. If you want your kids to be generous, give regularly to charity. Show them every day how you wish them to be.

Keep all these laws in their proper perspective by recalling the one law that rules them all: we have as much of a duty to fulfill their non-material needs—for love, discipline, guidance and belonging—as we do to fulfill their needs for food, medicine and shelter. For it is by these non-material gifts that we grant them safe passage into adulthood.

Give your kids credit, but I don't mean the revolving kind. Let them learn that happiness comes from their heads and not your wallet. Do the hard things that build character. Set reasonable expectations, give them responsibilities and opportunities to earn what they have, and hold them accountable for their actions. Have confidence in your children's capacity to handle life's challenges and let them do so, for it is just these very experiences that will help them grow and develop.

Psychologist Dan Kindlon in his research determined that children of families who ate dinner together a few times a week were less likely to get depressed, had less permissive attitudes toward sex, were less prone to drug abuse and were more likely to perform well in school. In his book, *Too Much of a Good Thing*, Kindlon tells how something as simple as having regular dinners or attending religious services together regularly went a long way toward encouraging open communication and mutual fun, the kind of glue that hold families together and gives kids the feeling of security needed for positive mental health.

If this doesn't sound like your family, what should you do? Set aside family time by scheduling dinners together, taking afternoon walks or time to play ball, setting up some fishing trips, helping with school projects, or going to church. Find things that your kids are interested in and get involved.

One amazing set of recent statistics compiled by Sandra Hofferth at the University of Michigan showed that time spent with family is becoming increasingly rare. Between 1981 and 1997, the amount of time families spent talking with one another declined dramatically.

There's no financial substitution to spending time together as a family. No amount of money and gifts can make up for the effects of long-term emotional neglect.

But spending time with our children and nurturing them is only half the job. It also means setting limits, putting boundaries up even when we know our kids will get angry, throw tantrums, and give us the silent treatment. It means pushing them to do things they may not want to do, standing up to them while providing the direction and structure they need in their lives. Give your kids what really counts, love and limits, something they can carry with them forever, long after your money runs out.

We've seen the struggles of affluent parents worried about their children growing up in the shadow of wealth. Such stories tell us in a poignant and unmistakable way that managing our money is no end in itself. It is only a means, a way for us to create wealth that we can share responsibly with our loved ones and others, a path to a life that offers true meaning and fulfillment. Money matters, but never for it's own sake.

No matter what our net worth may be, children are our most precious resource. So when the final bell tolls, every parent wants to know their children have the emotional, physical, financial, and spiritual resources to live a whole and satisfying life.

That is the golden legacy that no amount of money can buy.

References

Introduction

Haven, John and Schervish, Paul (1999) *Millionaires and the Millennium: New Estimates of the Forthcoming Wealth Transfer and the Prospects for the Golden Age of Philanthropy*, Boston: Social Welfare Research Institute.

Phillips, Kevin (1991) *The Politics of the Rich and Poor: Wealth and the American Electorate in the Reagan Aftermath*, New York: Harper-Collins.

Stanley, Thomas and Danko, William (1996), *The Millionaire Next Door.* New York: Pocket Books.

Allen, Michael (1987) *The Founding Fortunes: A New Anatomy of the Super-Rich Families in America*, New York: E.P. Dutton.

Chapter One

Wixen, Burton (1973) *The Children of the Rich.* New York: Crown Publishers.

O'Neill. Jessie (1997) *The Golden Ghetto: The Psychology of Affluence.* Center City, Minn: Hazeldon.

Bruccoli, Matthew (1995) *The Rich Boy*, In *Short Stories of F. Scott Fitzgerald.* New York: Scribner.

Nelson, Aldrich, (1996) *Old Money: The Mythology of Wealth in America.* Allworth Press.

Collier Peter and Horovitz, David (1994) *The Rockefellers*, New York: Blackstone.

Sedgewick, John, (1985) *Rich Kids.* New York: William Morrow.

Lebeau, Joyce (1988) The Silver Spoon Syndrome in the Super-Rich: the pathological linkage of affluence and narcissism in family systems. *American Journal of Psychotherapy.* 42, 425.

Coles, Robert (1977), *Children of Crisis, The Privileged Ones.* Boston: Little, Brown & Company.

Pittman, Frank (1987) *Turning Points: Treating Families in Transition.* New York: W.W. Norton.

Stanley, Thomas and Danko, William, *ibid.*

Chapter Two

Myers, David (1992) *The Pursuit of Happiness,* New York: Harper & Row.

Galbraith, John Kenneth (1998) *The Affluent Society.* New York: Houghlin Mifflin.

Chernow, Ron (1998) *Titan: The Life of John D. Rockefeller, Sr..* New York: Vintage Books.

Guiterrez, Gustavo (1985) *We Drink From Our Own Wells: The Spiritual Journey of a People.* Maryknoll, NY: Orbis Books.

Deiner, Edward (2000) *Culture and Subjective Well-Being: Well-Being and Quality of Life.* MIT Press.

Brandon, Nathaniel (1994) *The Six Pillars of Self-Esteem.* New York: Bantam Books.

Goleman, Daniel (1994) *Emotional Intelligence: Why It Can Matter More Than IQ.* New York: Bantam Books.

Chapter Four

Maslow, Abraham (1968) *Toward a Psychology of Being.* New York: Van Nostrand.

Chapter Five

Chernow, Ron, *ibid.*

Chapter Nine

Time/Cnn Poll (2002)

Godfrey, Neale (1995) *A Penny Saved: Teaching Your Children the Values and Life Skills They Will Need to Live in the Real World*. New York: Fireside Books.

Chapter Eleven

Aldrich, Nelson, *ibid*.

Edidin, P. (April, 1989) Drowning in wealth, *Psychology Today*, 34.

Chapter Twelve

Winokur, Jon (1996) *The Rich Are Different*. New York: Pantheon Books.

Buffone, Gary (2002) *The Myth of Tomorrow: Seven Keys for Living the Life You Want Today*. New York: McGraw-Hill.

Alexander, Michael (1998) *How to Inherit Money: A Guide to Making Good Financial Decisions After Losing Someone You Love*. Franklin Lakes, NJ: Career Press.

Crichton, Michael (1999) *Jurassic Park*. New York: Ballentine Books.

Chapter Thirteen

Baines, Barry (2001) *Ethical Wills: Putting Your Values on Paper*. New York: Perseus Press.

Pollan, Stephen and Mark Levine (1998) *Die Broke: A Radical Four Part Financial Plan*. New York: Harper Perennial.

Kindlon, Daniel (2001) *Too Much of a Good Thing: Raising Children of Character in an Indulgent Age*. New York: Miramax.

Appendix A

JUST WHAT IS FAMILY WEALTH COUNSELING?

A number of parents who worry how their good fortune will affect their kids feel a need to seek out professional guidance. I am often asked questions by both parents and financial professionals about this type of specialized consultation, a field now often referred to as family wealth counseling. Here are the most common questions and some brief responses.

Just what is family wealth counseling?

Actually the term can mean different things. For example, some financial and legal professionals are now using the title of "family wealth counselor" to describe what they do to help families who are facing difficult financial challenges. Although these professionals provide a range of valuable accounting, legal, and estate planning products and services, they are the first to admit that certain issues and problems fall well beyond their expertise and training. In fact, many of the people I see are referred from just such professionals.

Affluent families face certain unique emotional and psychological challenges that can greatly affect their health, happiness, and productivity. They may find themselves struggling over how they manage their finances, concerned about brat-proofing the young child, trying to motivate their underachieving adolescent, deciding on the best successor for the family business, refereeing sibling squabbles over inheritances, or making the difficult decisions on the distribution of their estates.

Just as difficult financial decisions require outside professional counsel, these complex, and often heart wrenching emotional issues are often best resolved with outside consultation as well. These concerns and counsel form the foundation for the specialized practice of the more psychologically-focused form of family wealth counseling that will be discussed here.

What's the difference between this and regular counseling?

Even though there is considerable overlap, the sub-specialization of family wealth counseling focuses more on the specific emotional and family issues and dynamics unique to more prosperous families and often, family businesses.

How does the process of family wealth counseling actually work?

There are several ways that a family wealth counselor can help. Some offer educational programs or seminars tailored to the specific needs of the family or family-owned company (i.e. resolving family conflict, improving communication, keys to successful succession or asset distribution).

Family wealth counselors can also be made part of the wealth management advisory team to help work through the complicated emotional issues or family dynamics that can block the constructive resolution of important problems. In this capacity the counselor works closely with the family and financial team members to help clarify and resolve the impasse.

Families can also contact and meet with a family wealth counselor privately, either in an office setting or in the comfort of their own home, to address their particular concerns.

Who is best qualified to provide such services?

Family wealth counselors should have two basic qualifications. First and foremost, they should be well trained and qualified to handle the most common emotional, psychological, and family issues that commonly arise. Minimally, these mental health professionals have advanced training and degrees and are licensed to practice in their state in the areas of psychology, psychiatry, family counseling or social work. But that training alone doesn't necessarily qualify them to work with high net-worth individuals.

Secondly, and as importantly, they should also have extensive experience in dealing with the special concerns of the affluent. Just as in choosing a financial or other professional, don't hesitate to call or meet with a prospective counselor and ask about their background and training, as well as their experience in dealing with problems of the affluent.

How do I find someone who is qualified to provide such a specialized service?

Talk with a friend or trusted advisor who may be able to refer you to a professional that can help you. This may be your trust officer, banker, accountant, attorney, financial planner, minister, therapist, or physician. If you can't locate a professional counselor who has specialized experience in working with the issues of affluenza in your area, many family wealth counselors provide consultative services telephonically, virtually through on-line contact, or they can travel to meet personally with a client.

What are the typical costs of such services?

The costs of these services will vary considerably depending on geography, the experience and training levels of the professional, as well as the particular kind of consultation offered. As with other professional services, rates are typically billed hourly or by service and in certain cases may be partially reimbursed by insurance.

What happens in the actual consultation meetings?

Typically, the counselor will begin by speaking with the client and/or financial advisors to better understand the specific family concern or issues. Once this is accomplished, the focus shifts to agreeing on goals and then designing and pursuing targeted interventions to address the identified concerns.

This can involve holding individual or family meetings, consultation with financial advisors or other professionals, offering educational programs and materials, focused vocational or psychological testing, or assigning specific homework to accomplish outside of the meetings. Of course, the type of follow-up depends entirely on the situation.

How long does something like this take?

It depends on the longevity and complexity of the problem. In most cases, this type of consultation is short-term and focused in nature and may only involve several meetings. In more involved situations such as with succession planning in the family business, consultation can be more extensive and lengthy.

Can I be assured of confidentiality?

Yes, but only if you see a professional who is licensed to practice their particular profession in their state, such as a psychologist, psychiatrist, or social worker. They are required by both state and federal law to maintain your information, whether verbal or written, as confidential unless you stipulate otherwise in writing through a signed release of information. For more information on the privacy protections available, go to www.byronharless.com.

What are some of the problems that can benefit from this type of consultation?

There are a number of issues that naturally arise with affluent families. These concerns include whether the children are properly motivated and are achieving their potential, whether they appropriately value money, are financially responsible and independent, and how they are reacting to the possibility of a large inheritance. Other issues involve parent or sibling conflicts over the family's business or assets, navigating the complex process of succession and passing on a family business, and developing appropriate trusts and asset transfers instruments to encourage healthy behavior while not damaging motivation, industry, and self-esteem. These are just a few examples.

Where can I learn more about this area?

Here are a few references that may be of interest to those wanting to learn more about the unique challenges facing the prosperous family.

Buffone, Gary W. *Choking on the Silver Spoon: Keeping Your Kids Healthy, Wealthy and Wise in a Land of Plenty.* Simplon Press, Spring 2004.

O'Neill, Jessie H., *The Golden Ghetto: The Psychology of Affluence.* Hazeldon, 1997, go to The Affluenza Project for additional resources at www.affluenza.com.

Gallo, Ellen & Gallo, Jon. *Silver Spoon Kids.* McGraw-Hill, 2002.

This information excerpted from "The Ten Most Commonly Asked Questions on Family Wealth Counseling," by Gary W. Buffone in *The Psychology of Prosperity* Series, to be released from Simplon Press, Summer 2004. For more information visit www.psychologythatworks.com.

APPENDIX B

MORE ON THE FAMILY'S BUSINESS

Nearly 85% of businesses are family owned or operated, and the inherent conflicts in that mixture of blood and business are inevitable. Here are a few basic tips for parents and adult children who are facing these difficult challenges every day.

CLEARLY DEFINE THE VALUES AND MISSION. Sit down with the key players, family members and otherwise, and be sure to discuss and define the core values and mission of the organization. This needs to be done early and with rapidly growing companies, regularly. Be sure everyone's on board.

ORGANIZE THE FAMILY AND BUSINESS. Establish a well-defined governance structure for decision-making, priority setting, policy-making, role and job definitions, and running the business. Whether this be an executive committee or outside Board of Directors, make sure the roles and responsibilities of the member are clearly outlined and lines of authority and control clear. In well run family businesses, the roles and functions of the family, board, and management are distinct, yet mutually supportive and complimentary.

HOLD FAMILY MEETINGS. Communicate, communicate, and communicate. It is critical that regular and effective family meetings be held to provide members the opportunity to discuss issues in a timely fashion, thereby preventing larger problems down the road. These meetings are one of the most important steps business owners can take to ensure the continuity and success of the family business. Run well, these meetings strengthen the family and business by giving members a chance to develop skills in public speaking, leadership, teaching and conflict resolution. Issues covered can include succession, compensation, participation and ownership, accountability, hiring and firing and harmony.

START SUCCESSION PLANNING EARLY. One of the biggest reasons family businesses fail is poor succession planning. Less than a third of family businesses survive into the second generation and well less than a fifth make it into the third generation. As uncomfortable a topic as succession is, get it on the table and planning started. Successful transitions can take anywhere from 3 to 15 years to complete and are fraught with obstacles. Start as soon as possible.

These suggestions are general in nature and are offered as food for thought. Clearly, many of the challenges faced by family-owned companies are often complex and some require outside consultation. If you happen to consult a family business center, here are some of the ways they may be able to assist your family and business:

Helping families articulate their values, history and culture in development of mission

Assisting in strategic planning and holding effective family meetings

Assessing family and business strengths and developmental needs

Building and improving family communication skills

Evaluating key personnel for selection and management development

Coaching and educating family members on the consequences of wealth

Helping siblings with conflict resolution and developing teamwork

Counseling family members for career development

Succession planning and process consultation

For more information on family businesses and related issues, consult *The Family Business Magazine* at www.familybusinessmagazine.com or visit our web site at www.byronharless.com.

Resources

Books

Argyle, Michael, *The Psychology of Happiness,* Routledge.

Ashner, Laurie and Mitch Meyerson, *When Is Enough, Enough? What You Can Do If You Never Feel Satisfied,* Hazelden Publishing Company.

Baker, Dan, *What Happy People Know: How the New Science of Happiness Can Change Your Life for the Better,* Rodale Press.

Blouin, Barbara with Katherine Gibson and Margaret Kiersted, *The Legacy of Inherited Wealth: Interviews with Heirs,* The Inheritance Project.

Brill, Hal, Jack A. Brill, and Cliff Feigenbaum, *Investing With Your Values: Making Money & Making a Difference,* Bloomberg Press.

Brill, Jack A. and Alan Reder, *Investing From The Heart: A Guide to Socially Responsible Investments & Money Management,* Crown Publishers.

Brock, Henry S., *Your Complete Guide to Money Happiness,* Legacy, Inc.

Brown, Frederick S., *Money & Spirit,* A.R.E. Press.

Carlson, Richard, *Don't Sweat the Small Stuff About Money: Spiritual and Practical Ways to Create Abundance and More Fun in Your Life,* Hyperion.

Collins, Chuck and Pam Rogers with Joan P. Garner, *Robin Hood Was Right: A Guide to Giving Your Money for Social Change,* W.W. Norton & Company.

Condon, Gerald M. & Jeffrey L. Condon, *Beyond the Grave: The Right Way & the Wrong Way of Leaving Money to Your Children,* Harper Business.

Furnham, Adrian and Michael Argyle, *The Psychology of Money,* Routledge.

Hacker, Andrew, *Money: Who Has How Much and Why*, Scribner.

Kiyosaki, Robert T. and Sharon L. Lechter, *Rich Dad, Poor Dad: What the Rich Teach Their Kids About Money That the Poor and Middle Class Do Not!*, Warner Books.

Lermitte, Paul W. and Jennifer Merritt, *Making Allowances: A Dollars and Sense Guide to Teaching Kids About Money*, McGraw-Hill.

Le Van, Gerald, *Raising Rich Kids*, Xlibris Corporation.

Link, E.G., *Getting to the Heart of the Matter: A Revolution in Estate Planning for Wealthy Families* Indiana, Professional Mentoring Program.

Madanes, Cloe and Claudio Madanes, *The Secret Meaning of Money*, Jossey-Bass.

Minear, Dr. Ralph E. and William Proctor, *Kids Who Have Too Much: Does Your Child Really Need "The Best of Everything"*, Thomas Nelson Publishers.

Needleman, Jacob, *Money and the Meaning of Life*, Currency-Doubleday.

Needleman, Jacob, Michael Toms, Marsha Sinetar, and Lynne Twist, *Money, Money, Money: The Search for Wealth and the Pursuit of Happiness*, Hay House.

Nemeth, Ph.D., Maria, *The Energy of Money: The Spiritual Guide to Financial and Personal Fulfillment*, Ballentine Wellspring.

Nemeth, Ph.D., Maria, *You and Money: Would It Be All Right With You If Life Got Easier?*, Vildehiya Publications.

Phillips, Michael, *The Seven Laws of Money*, Shambhala.

Samalin, Nancy and Catherine Whitney, *Loving without Spoiling: And 100 Other Timeless Tips for Raising Terrific Kids*, McGraw-Hill.

Schervish, Paul G., Platon E. Coursoukis, and Ethan Lewis, *Gospels of Wealth: How the Rich Portray Their Lives*, Praeger Publishers.

Slepian, Anne and Christopher Mogil, *We Gave Away a Fortune*, New Society Publishers.

Williams, Roy O., *For Love & Money*, Monterey Pacific Institute.

Organizations

The Inheritance Project

This organization provides information, publications and consulting to help people explore the emotional and social impact of inherited wealth.

The Inheritance Project
6940 Tupper Grove Halifax, NS B3H2M6 Canada
Phone: 902-431-8890 Fax: 902-429-0040
www.inheritance-project.com

The Philanthropic Initiative

This is one of a number of groups that works and consults with family and corporate fund-raisers who are attempting to donate funds in a more strategic manner.

77 Franklin Street, Boston, MA 02110
617-338-2590, Fax: 617-338-2591
www.tpi.org
get2us@tpi.org

Alternatives for Simple Living

Begun in 1973 to take a stand against the over-commercialization of Christmas, the focus of this organization is on empowering people to take steps toward voluntary simplicity by changing oneself, sharing with others, and changing larger systems, like businesses and governments. Alternatives is a non-profit organization that equips people of faith to challenge rampant consumerism, live justly, and celebrate responsibly.

5312 Morningside Avenue, P.O. Box 2857, Sioux City, Iowa 51106
1-800-821-6153
www.simpleliving.org
alternatives@simpleliving.org

Center for the New American Dream

The Center is a not-for-profit membership-based organization that helps individuals, families, and institutions reduce and shift consumption as a way to enhance our quality of life and help protect the environment.

6930 Carroll Avenue, Suite 900, Takoma Park, MD 20912
301-891-ENUF (3683), 877-68-DREAM, Fax: 301-891-3684
www.newdream.org
newdream@newdream.org

Index

P

Philanthropy 72, 133, 164, 173
Pillsbury, George 15
Pittman, Frank 17
Pollan, Stephen 171
Positive parenting in the age of abundance 1
Private foundations 173, 174
Probate 4, 141, 158
Psychologists 4, 5, 23, 24, 29, 30, 48, 112, 144, 149, 150, 168, 178

R

Randall, Michael 138
Resilience 36, 39, 58, 59, 60, 64, 103, 176
Rich kidís disease 45
Rockefeller xvii, 7, 29, 59, 77, 158
Rockefeller, John D. 29, 59, 77
Roper survey 24

S

Schervish, Paul xvi, 20
School of hard knocks 125, 126, 128
Sedgewick, John 7
Self-control 32, 33, 35, 56, 103, 176
Self-efficacy 30
Self-esteem xviii, 13, 15, 16, 30, 35, 38, 39, 40, 57, 59, 108, 111, 121, 125, 131, 132, 153, 155, 156
Self-respect 30
Self-worth 13, 15, 28, 37, 40, 48, 73, 111, 113, 133, 177
Seligman, Martin 24
Seneca 29
Silver Spoon Syndrome 5, 8, 9, 10, 13, 34, 35, 37, 41, 65, 93, 95, 113, 144
Silver spooner 9, 10, 11, 12, 14, 15, 16, 17, 19, 20, 21, 33, 71, 72, 139, 163
Slater, Phillip 105, 110
Social class 17
Spooners 11, 12, 14, 15, 16, 17, 18, 19, 20, 21, 30, 31, 35, 122, 139, 163
Stanley, Thomas 20, 27
Stephens, Jackson 154

Stone, Michael 133
Substance abuse 16, 19, 21, 38, 115
Supportive refusal 58

T

Trust 13, 31, 89, 126, 133, 134, 142, 143, 145, 151, 152, 154, 157, 161, 162, 163, 164, 165, 166, 167, 168, 169, 170, 171, 172, 173, 174
Trustee 152, 161, 162, 163, 164, 165, 166, 167, 173

U

Underachievement 8, 11, 37, 38, 46, 47, 120, 121
Underachievers 111, 121
Unstable relationships 14

V

Values 9, 10, 13, 19, 27, 28, 33, 36, 37, 40, 59, 77, 83, 85, 86, 87, 88, 89, 95, 97, 102, 134, 142, 159, 161, 177
Vanderbilt, Arthur 157

W

Wills 89, 156, 157, 161, 162, 168, 169, 175
Winokur, Jon 139
Wisdom 31, 32, 33, 35, 166, 171
Wixen, Burton 7
Work ethic xviii, xix, 31, 164

This book was set in
Minion and Adobe Garamond types
by Angela Werner

Give the Gift of Positive Financial Parenting!

Order extra copies of:
Choking on the Silver Spoon:
Keeping Your Kids Healthy, Wealthy and Wise in a Land of Plenty

☐ YES, I want _____ copies of **Choking on the Silver Spoon** at $19.95 each plus $4.00 shipping and handling per book (Georgia residents please add 6% sales tax - $1.20) Allow 15 days for delivery.

My check or money order for $_____.___ is enclosed.

Please charge my credit card:
MasterCard ☐ VISA ☐ American Express ☐ Discover ☐

Card # _____ *Exp. Date* _____

Signature _____

Name _____

Address _____

City/State/Zip _____

Phone _____ *E-mail* _____

Please make your check payable to and return to:

BookMasters, Inc.
PO Box 388
Ashland, OH 44805

Or order by:

Phone: Toll-Free – 800-247-6553

Fax: 419 - 281 - 6883

E-mail: order@bookmaster.com

You may also purchase the book on-line from Amazon, Barnes & Noble, Borders and other on-line retailers.

Give the Gift of Positive Financial Parenting!

Order extra copies of:
Choking on the Silver Spoon:
Keeping Your Kids Healthy, Wealthy and Wise in a Land of Plenty

☐ YES, I want _____ copies of **Choking on the Silver Spoon** at $19.95 each plus $4.00 shipping and handling per book (Georgia residents please add 6% sales tax - $1.20) Allow 15 days for delivery.

My check or money order for $_____.____ is enclosed.

Please charge my credit card:
MasterCard ☐   VISA ☐   American Express ☐   Discover ☐

Card # _____ *Exp. Date* _____

Signature _____

Name _____

Address _____

City/State/Zip _____

Phone _____ *E-mail* _____

Please make your check payable to and return to:

BookMasters, Inc.
PO Box 388
Ashland, OH 44805

Or order by:

Phone: Toll-Free – 800-247-6553

Fax: 419 - 281 - 6883

E-mail: order@bookmaster.com

You may also purchase the book on-line from Amazon, Barnes & Noble, Borders and other on-line retailers.